In Sickness and in
Askrigg Equitable, Benevolent,
1809-2000

Cover photograph: Askrigg Friendly Society Flag held by the Colour Bearers,
Mason Scarr and James Scarr

To all the men, past, present and future, of the
Askrigg Friendly Society

In Sickness and in Health

Askrigg Equitable, Benevolent, and Friendly Society 1809-2000

Christine Hallas

William Sessions Limited
York, England

© Christine Hallas 2000

ISBN 1 85072 258 7

Printed by Sessions of York
The Ebor Press
York, England

Contents

Introduction		ix
Chapter 1	Beginnings	1
Chapter 2	Membership	5
Chapter 3	Articles of the Society	19
Chapter 4	Finances of the Society	31
Chapter 5	In Sickness…	53
Chapter 6	…and in Health	71
Chapter 7	Past, Present and Future	83

Appendices
1. Early members of the AEBFS, 1809-11 — 87
2. Articles of the AEBFS, 1832 — 88
3. Presidents of the AEBFS, 1820-2000 — 93
4. Valuation Report, 1890 — 95
5. Valuation of Shaw Farm, Lunds, 1901 — 96
6. Place, date and cause of death of selected members — 97
7. Garland Day Sports — 100
8. Askrigg Friendly Society Sports, 1924 — 101

Identification of AEBFS members in photographs — 102

Bibliography and Further Reading — 103

Acknowledgements

I am indebted to many people who have provided material and given me support in producing this book. They are too numerous to mention all individually but my thanks are due, particularly to Marie Hartley and Joan Ingilby who wrote *Yorkshire Village*, to Mary Halton who took the photographs of the procession, and to Askrigg Friendly Society members, particularly Tucker Metcalfe, Bill Thwaite, Edgar Daykin, Bob Petty, Peter Thompson and Allen Kirkbride.

This book is part of a much larger research project into self-help in the nineteenth century and I am grateful for the support and assistance of colleagues at Trinity and All Saints, University of Leeds, particularly Sylvia Simpson and the staff of the General Office, and Nikki Smith. My thanks are also due to Claire Harvey, Jacqui White and Steve Viles who, as part of their undergraduate dissertations, undertook some analysis of the material and made textual observations, some of which are included here.

Finally, the book would not have been written without the help and support of my husband, George, who also proof read the text.

Askrigg Friendly Society is grateful to the Yorkshire Rural Community Council for a grant towards the cost of publishing this book.

Introduction

During the late eighteenth and nineteenth centuries life in Britain underwent a dramatic change as industrialization and population increase affected both town and country dwellers. The consequent upheavals meant that the traditional paternalistic approach towards the poor and their rights to assistance was replaced by a much harsher regime.

Under the 1601 Poor Law Act, parish support had been given to those who applied for poor relief and the costs were met by local ratepayers. However, by 1800, increased population and attendant pauperism saw the cost of poor relief escalate and payment of the rapidly rising poor rate was increasingly resented by ratepayers. The 1601 Act was no longer considered adequate but debate as to what should replace it was fierce and it was not until the 1830s that new legislation was introduced. The 1834 Poor Law Amendment Act established Poor Law Unions throughout the country and laid down the principle that parish relief was to be given only to workhouse inmates. The Union Workhouses, which became known as 'Bastilles', were regarded with dread by ordinary working people and, in order to protect themselves against pauperism, many individuals tried to ensure that they had a buffer against hard times. In the pre-industrial past, craft guilds had generally provided some support to their members but from 1687, when the Bethnal Green Friendly Society was formed, a new model of self-help was introduced.

Although many friendly societies were established during the eighteenth century, it was only from the 1790s, when the problems of poverty, and the increased burden of poor relief, became acute, that the number of friendly societies and their membership expanded rapidly. It is estimated that by 1800 there were over 7,000 friendly societies in England and Wales with a total membership of between 6-700,000. Given that there were only 8.8 million people in England and Wales in 1801, friendly societies were providing insurance against destitution to a significant proportion of the population. In the North Riding of Yorkshire alone, in 1802-3, there were 69 societies with 9,719 members. The friendly society movement reached its zenith in the nineteenth century. In 1818 there were over 920,000 members in the country and, by 1850, the figure had risen to one and a half million. By the 1890s, when the population of England and Wales was 29 million, friendly society membership stood at approximately four million. In other words, at the end of the nineteenth century almost 14 per cent of the population, together with their families, had the insurance of friendly society membership.

Two main types of friendly society developed. The earlier societies were independent and locally based but, as the movement rapidly expanded from the late eighteenth century, nationally-based societies sprang up. The national societies, such as the 'Ancient Order of Buffaloes' and the 'Independent Order of Oddfellows', with their local affiliated lodges throughout the country, became the dominant type of society by the mid-nineteenth century and the number of independent societies declined. In 1874 it was noted that, although there had been about 3,200 friendly societies in Yorkshire in 1802-3, the figure had fallen to c1,500 by 1870. Most of these were lodges of affiliated societies. Only 212 independent, locally-based societies survived in Yorkshire in 1870 and of these only 42 had funds in excess of £1,000. Many of the smaller, independent societies were unable to withstand competition from the affiliated lodges and by 1900 most had disappeared.

Throughout the nineteenth century, unless they had insurance, those who fell on hard times had to suffer the indignity of the 'pauper' system and its harsh workhouse requirements. However, by the end of the nineteenth century attitudes towards poverty were changing and, although the poor law system survived until 1929, proposals for the payment of state old-age pensions were under consideration. By the early twentieth century, the original pension proposals were extended to provide state support for sickness and unemployment. These proposals were formally enacted in the 1908 Old Age Pension Act and Lloyd George's radical 1911 National Insurance Act. The 1911 Act required workers to pay national insurance and, in return, they were entitled to sickness and unemployment benefit.

It has been suggested that the 1908 and 1911 Acts presaged the demise of friendly societies. This is not quite true. The new government measures provided only limited and, generally, inadequate benefits. Although other forms of self-help, such as building societies, savings clubs and co-operative societies, were available, the more prudent individuals preferred to keep some additional form of insurance. However, by the early twentieth century, it is clear that the movement had passed its heyday and membership was in decline, a decline which was accelerated by Sir William Beveridge's 1942 report. This report formed the foundation of the Labour Party's welfare state initiative and resulted in the Insurance Act of 1946. At the same time Aneurin Bevan established the National Health Service which was intended to provide support 'from cradle to grave'. This legislation sounded the death knell for many of the remaining friendly societies, particularly the independent ones, although a few survived and, in some cases, flourished.

While the threat of pauperism, which had encouraged the establishment of friendly societies over the last two hundred years, has largely disappeared, those societies that have survived continue to serve a valuable, though largely social, function within their communities. This is particularly true of the few remaining independent societies in rural areas. Although at the beginning of the twenty-first century, most people would see friendly societies as having little value outside their communities, attitudes are again changing. In the light of recent discussion concerning privately-funded pensions and the future of the National Health Service, it may be that self-help, rather than full reliance on state care, will assume a new importance. This might in turn lead to a revival in the fortunes of friendly societies.

Chapter 1

Beginnings

> Whereas all Men are liable to various Accidents and Misfortunes, which during their continuance, may deprive them of the Capacity of their own subsistence; for the Purpose of Alleviating all such Accidents and Misfortunes, that may happen to any of Us, whose Names are hereunto subscribed, We do hereby voluntarily associate ourselves by the Name of the WENSLEYDALE UNION SOCIETY, and engage to be subject to the following Orders and Regulations.
>
> *Rules of the Wensleydale Union Society, 1774*

By the end of the eighteenth century, and in common with other areas of the country, Wensleydale was experiencing a rapid rise in population. The pressure on the local economy was particularly acute in upper Wensleydale. Here the poor rate rose steeply and in 1802-3 was 12s 2d per head which was double the average for the North Riding of Yorkshire and significantly higher than the England and Wales figure of 8s 11d. The economic problems afflicting the area were also reflected in heavy out-migration. Between 1801 and 1811 Wensleydale lost 18 per cent of its population through out-migration as people tried to escape the poverty resulting from decreasing employment opportunities. As Charles Fothergill, who visited Wensleydale in 1805, noted:

> Many of the poor families in this dale are so numerous...that the country is not able to find support for all the inhabitants, insomuch that a great part of the youth when old enough are compelled to migrate. (P. Romney, ed., *The Diary of Charles Fothergill 1805*, Leeds, 1981, pp.110-1.)

In confronting these pressures, the ratepayers of Askrigg Township took the decision to join with eight other townships in upper Wensleydale and Swaledale and form a Poor Law Union under the permissive terms of Gilbert's Act of 1782. A new workhouse was built at Bainbridge in 1809-10 and the Bainbridge (later known as Aysgarth) Union came into force in 1812. This Union was much more humane than those created elsewhere in the country under the mandatory requirements of the Poor Law Amendment Act of 1834.

The people of upper Wensleydale saw the new Bainbridge Union as only one part of their fight against poverty and rising poor rates. Local people did not want to be reliant solely on central authorities or the poor law, they wished to remain independent, staving off poverty by providing for themselves and their families either through their employment or through self-help insurance.

Township Map of Wensleydale and Swaledale

Friendly societies were not new to the area. The Wensleydale Union Society had been established in 1774. James Lightfoot, an Askrigg apothecary, was the first President and James Brougham and William Terry were the Stewards. The Wensleydale Union Society met at the George Public House in Askrigg. By 1802-3 Reeth and Middleham each had two societies and there were societies in Arkengarthdale and in Preston-under-Scar. However, these early societies attracted variable support. While there was a total of 173 and 320 friendly society members in Reeth and Middleham respectively, the Preston Friendly Society had only 10 members. Although the Wensleydale Union Society had 106 members, it was evidently not thriving financially and by 1809 appeared to have been defunct. Given the impending creation of the Bainbridge Union, the inhabitants of Askrigg felt that they needed their own self-help solution and so the 'Askrigg Equitable, Benevolent, and Friendly Society' (AEBFS) was established on 4 March 1809.[1] From its inception the Society was known locally as 't'Club'. The first names on the subscription list of the new society were Joseph and John Lodge who had been instrumental in the establishment of the Society. Joseph Lodge was keen for the Society to succeed and gave £5 at the first meeting. He had bought the King's Arms Hotel in c1800 and had subsequently built the adjoining Assembly Rooms, where he allowed the upper room to be used by the Society as its 'Club Room'.

At the first meeting of the Askrigg Society 25 people paid 3s 6d to join and some gave an extra donation to help build up the funds. Others quickly joined and by the end of 1809 the Society had 43 members (see Table 1.1 for details of founder members). By 1812, when the Bainbridge Poor Law Union came into being, the AEBFS had 72 members. The Society continued to be successful and in 1815 it was the only surviving society of any significance in Wensleydale. In that year a return to the national Friendly Society Registry showed that the AEBFS had a total of 148 members.[2] The Askrigg Society grew in strength throughout the nineteenth century, successfully achieving its aims by protecting its members against unemployment, illness and the spectre of pauperism. In the 1890s the local vicar, the Rev. Christopher Whaley, proudly claimed that, since its inception, the Society had spent over £10,000 on benefits and not one of its members had ever had to claim poor relief.[3]

---

1 The name has changed slightly over the years. For example, in the 1999 Annual Return the Society is referred to as the Askrigg Equitable and Benevolent Society.
2 In 1815 the only other society in Wensleydale was at High Abbotside and had eight members. Swaledale was better served. In addition to the Reeth and Arkengarthdale societies, a new society with 64 members was formed at Melbecks. All these societies declined, however, and by 1851 only the AEBFS was registered.
3 This was not quite true as at least one member claimed poor relief. Jeffrey Dinsdale, a tailor who had joined the Society in 1809, claimed poor relief

Table 1.1

Founder Members of AEBFS, March 1809

Age	Members Names	Abode	Occupation
48	Joseph Lodge	Askrigg	Brewer
45	John Lodge	Askrigg	Attorney
58	James Pratt	Grange	Mason
51	Edward Thompson	Askrigg	Joiner
32	George Bell	Askrigg	Joiner
43	James Scarr	Helm	Mason
46	Richard Mason	Askrigg	Farmer
40	Robert Cloughton	Askrigg	Farmer
33	Thomas Butson	Stonesdale	Joiner
26	Clement Bell	New Park	Joiner
38	George Scarr	Luke's House	Farmer
48	John Teasdale	Askrigg	Cordwainer
47	Francis Shepherd	Askrigg	Labourer
58	Jeffrey Dinsdale Sen.	Askrigg	Tailor
20	Francis Thompson	Askrigg	Joiner
28	Eldad Milner	Askrigg	Miller
29	Edmund Dixon	Longrigg	Farmer
32	William Cleasby	Scartop	Servant
30	William Metcalfe	New Houses	Labourer
26	Jeffrey Dinsdale Jnr.	New Park (Askrigg)	Tailor
22	William Trotter	Askrigg	Servant
25	Samuel Sykes	Askrigg	Grocer
38	Anthony Storey	Askrigg	Cordwainer
25	John Thwaite	Thwaite Holm	Slater
22	John Woodward	Askrigg	Badger

Source: AEBFS, 2/1, Book of Members, 1809-81.

during the last years of his life. On his death in 1863, the Askrigg Poor Law Guardian claimed, and received, the Society's funeral allowance which was normally paid to the deceased's next-of-kin.

Chapter 2

Membership

The initial enthusiasm for joining the AEBFS was largely maintained in the ensuing years. However, there were periods when interest waned and, as a consequence, the membership profile of the Society has changed significantly during the 190 years of its existence. In order to understand the significance of membership levels and to gain as full a picture as possible of the Society, both total membership over the whole period and the number registered at any one time are examined. In addition, the changing structure of the Society is identified by examining the proportion of both new and total members in different age categories, and by analysing the occupations and status of members.

Size of Membership

Between its creation in 1809 and the end of 1999, 953 individuals have been members of the Society. These comprised both ordinary members and honorary members. Although these two categories of membership were not enshrined in the Society's Articles until 1876, there have been, in effect, two types of member from the earliest days.[1] The main difference between the two categories is that honorary members make an annual donation (usually not less than the contributions of ordinary members) and do not draw any benefits from the Society. In contrast, ordinary (sometimes known as 'benefit') members paid quarterly contributions and received sickness and other benefits when needed. Throughout the nineteenth century the great majority of new entrants were ordinary members. For example, of the 362 members who had joined between 1809 and 1873 it appears that only 43 were honorary members. In June 1874, J.J. Thwaite, Gentleman of Nappa Hall, Askrigg became the first honorary member to be officially accorded that title in the Members Book. However, as early as 1820 'honorary mem-

---

1 Honorary members were mentioned briefly in the 1832 Articles but were not identified as a specific category of member until 1876.

bers' were mentioned in the minutes of meetings. In the twentieth century, the balance between ordinary and honorary members changed and by the end of the century a high proportion of those joining the Society did so as honorary members. For example, 50 per cent (36 of 72) of new entrants in the 1980s were honorary members and in the 1990s the proportion had risen to 55 per cent (47 of 86). This rise in the proportion of honorary members reflects, in part, an increase in the number of 'incomers' in the community and, through an interest in local tradition, in membership of the Society.

AEBFS Honorary Members and Subscriptions, 1876-81

Although it is often difficult to ascertain the membership at any one date, particularly in the early years of the Society, extant evidence does provide the occasional snapshot. Table 2.1 shows that the total number of members at any one time varied significantly over the 190 years of the Society's existence. For example, numbers fell from 148 in 1815 to 60 in 1828 before rising again to 123 in 1881.

Table 2.1

AEBFS Membership at selected dates 1809-2000

	O.M.[1]	H.M.[2]	Total		O.M.[1]	H.M.[2]	Total
1809			25	1919	56		
1815			148	1929	46		
1819	100	4	104	1935	58		
1828	53	7	60	1944	47		
1858	94	15	109	1954	69		
1863			118	1964	94		
1871	103			1974	133		
1881	111	12	123	1984	124	32	156
1890	104			1992	136		
1900	97			2000	118	67	185

[1] Ordinary Members.
[2] Honorary Members.
Note: The records sometimes return only the number of ordinary members and, on occasions, just the total members (honorary and ordinary).
Source: AEBFS, 2/1, 2/8, Books of Members, 1809-81 and 1881-2000.

Although in the mid-nineteenth century the level of membership looked relatively healthy, the survival of the Society was by no means assured. By the 1850s several of the national societies had established lodges in the area and were in direct competition with the AEBFS. For example, a lodge of the Independent Order of Oddfellows had been established in 1837 at West Burton and by 1847 had over 100 members. Similarly, Leyburn had a branch of this Society by the 1860s. In 1863, Leyburn also had a branch of the 'Heart of Oak Provident' with 59 members and funds of £158. In 1859, a lodge of the United Order of the Golden Fleece was formed at West Witton with 28 founder members. There were also new local independent societies. The Loyal Dales Independent Friendly Society was formed in 1865 and had branches in Swaledale and Arkengarthdale. By 1874 the Loyal Dales Society had 140 members. These societies probably adversely affected the AEBFS which drew its membership not only from Askrigg but from a large part of upper Wensleydale.

The number of ordinary members reached a nineteenth century peak of 111 in 1881. Thereafter, the AEBFS membership started to decline and it looked as though the Society might suffer the fate of many other small societies. Although there were still 104 ordinary members in 1908, numbers had fallen to 85 by 1911. A further significant fall in membership took place in the period of the First World War. By 1919 the number of ordinary members had declined to 56 and fell further to 46 in 1929. Despite efforts to stem the decline, there were still only 58 ordinary members in 1935. It appears, therefore, that the Society reached its nadir in the first half of the twentieth century and may have come close to termination. However, particularly after the Second World War, efforts to increase membership met with some success and by 1964 ordinary membership had crept back up to 94. The rise continued and by 1984, with 124 ordinary members and 32 honorary members, the Society was looking increasingly healthy. This trend has been maintained and, by 2000, total membership had risen to 185.

Numbers of New Members

The long-term vitality of a friendly society can probably be best gauged from its success in recruiting new members. Perhaps, not surprisingly, the number of new members joining the AEBFS in each decade varied enormously. After an initial high of 93 in its first decade, registrations slipped to 14 in 1820-9 (see Appendix 1 for early members). Thereafter, recruitment settled down and generally ranged between 32 and 52 new members per decade. The early twentieth century witnessed a marked decline in the intake of new members, with only 21 joining in 1900-9. However, the Society was extremely resilient and actively sought to recruit new, particularly young, members. It was so successful that between 1950 and 1959 47 new members joined and, as the century advanced, the Society went from strength to strength. In the period 1980-9 the Society gained 72 new members and in 1990-9 attracted 80 new members, the latter representing the highest level of new recruits since the Society's inaugural decade. However, many of the recent members are honorary so the Society is currently seeking to rectify the imbalance. As the AEBFS entered the new millennium, it was once again actively encouraging local young men to join as ordinary members.

Age of Members

The age of new members is important for any friendly society as it is from young people, with a long working life ahead of them, that a society's funds are drawn. In view of this, most societies, including the AEBFS, have a strict upper age limit for new members. However, as its initial priority was to build its membership base, the Askrigg Society did not impose an age limit in its first year of existence. This resulted in men as old as 58 years joining the Society. Subsequently, lower and upper age limits of 16 and 30 years for new ordinary members were rigorously enforced.[2] These age limits pertained until the early twentieth century when, reflecting increased life expectancy and in order to boost membership, the upper age limit for new members was raised to 45 years.

As might be expected, the average age of new members was highest (27.5 years) in the first decade of the Society's existence. Thereafter, the average age of new members declined, settling at around 22 years in the 1860s. In the next decade the average age at entry rose slightly to 24 years and this average was maintained for over a hundred years. Even in the late twentieth century the average age of 25 years represents only a slight rise from the 1870s figure.

The actual age of all (new and established) members at any point in time has a significant bearing on a society's financial well-being. There had to be enough men in the relatively healthy age range of 20 to 50 years who were in work, who were less likely to call upon the society's resources, and who could afford to pay subscriptions at a high enough level to support benefits for sickness, old age and death of other less robust or elderly members.

---

[2] There was no age limit for new honorary members and so their age was not normally recorded in the Members Book.

Extract from AEBFS Members Book 1809-81

Although substantial numbers of local people left the dales throughout the nineteenth century, the flow of migration was particularly heavy in the 1880s and 1890s. Difficulties in farming, loss of employment opportunities and the attraction of other areas were powerful forces and inclined many to leave the area. As the migrants were usually the young and healthy, this altered the age profile of the Society. The increasing proportion of older members from the late nineteenth century onward meant that the number of members in receipt of benefits exceeded those paying subscriptions. The high level of outgoings, coupled with relatively low levels of income, increasingly threatened the viability of the Society. The response to the situation in the early part of the twentieth century was to seek to increase honorary membership. However, this was a short-term solution and it was clear that more young ordinary members were needed. By 1924 the situation was dire as the Society had no members under the age of 30. Almost half the members were over 60 years old, a fifth were over 70 years and two men were over 85 years old. The AEBFS strove to recruit more young people and by 1934 had partly succeeded. However, although some younger men had joined, Table 2.2 shows that the age profile of all members was still heavily biased towards the more elderly.

Table 2.2

Age profile of all ordinary members of the Society in 1934

Age	16-25 yrs	26-35 yrs	36-50 yrs	51-65 yrs	over 65 yrs	Total
Members	10	8	11	9	12	52

Source: AEBFS, 2/8, Book of Members, 1881-2000.

The objective of attracting sufficient young men as ordinary members was not really achieved until after World War II. Only when the country began to emerge from the austerity of the war years did the AEBFS's drive to attract new members achieve significant success. Over the ensuing decades the age profile of ordinary members slowly improved so that, by the 1980s, the Society had regained a much healthier age balance. As Table 2.3 shows, most of those joining in the 1980s were under 30 years old despite the fact that the upper age limit was 45 years. Unfortunately, during the 1990s there has been a shift once again in the age profile towards the older age range.

Table 2.3

Age profile of new ordinary members 1980-89

Age	16-19 yrs	20-24 yrs	25-29 yrs	30-34 yrs	Over 35 yrs	Total
Members	9	8	10	5	3	35

Note: 1980-9 = 36 new ordinary members. The age of one new member was not recorded.
Source: As Table 2.2.

Askrigg Friendly Society members, c1880 J.B. Smithson
(for details see p.102)

Occupations of Members

From the Society's inception its occupational profile has virtually mirrored that of the upper Wensleydale community and was very similar to that of many other rural, particularly upland, areas. Almost every local occupation was represented, the exceptions being those jobs that were specific to women. The professions were represented by solicitor/attorney, doctor/surgeon, clergyman, teacher, bank manager and 'druggist' (pharmacist). Crafts included such occupations as stone mason, slater, joiner, cordwainer, tailor, glazier, sadler, blacksmith, painter, engineer, shoemaker, watchmaker, and cooper. The trades and services were represented by diverse occupations such as draper, upholsterer, butcher, badger (corn dealer), miller, grocer, greengrocer, fish merchant, carrier, tallow chandler, plumber, electrician, inn keeper and hotelier. Other occupations represented were miner/collier, textile worker (yarn spinner, weaver, and hosier), postman, ambulance driver, policeman, draughtsman, gamekeeper, haulage contractor, garage proprietor, motor driver, workhouse master, highway surveyor, auctioneer and revenue officer. After the arrival of the railway in Wensleydale in 1878, several new members of the Society were recorded as having rail-related occupations. These included railway clerk, railway guard, railway porter and platelayer.

The membership records of the AEBFS show that its occupational profile, over the 190 years of its existence, was not static. Although some traditional occupations have survived, many have disappeared and been replaced by new activities which reflect the considerable economic and social change that has taken place over the Society's lifetime. Tables 2.4 to 2.7 demonstrate the substantial changes that have occurred in the significance of the major occupational groups over the period.[3]

Table 2.4

Occupational Categories of New Members 1809-49

Occupational Category	No. of Members	%
Gentleman	16	7.0
Professional	13	5.6
Farmer	23	10.0
Trades/Services	36	15.7
Skilled workers	65	28.3
Servant/Unskilled worker	30	13.0
Labourer	38	16.5
Miner	9	3.9
Total	230	100.0

Notes:
1 Although 'Gentleman' is not strictly an occupational category it is included here as it was recorded under the 'occupation' column in the Book of Members.
2 The occupations of a few members were missing.
Source: AEBFS 2/1, Book of Members, 1809-81.

The distribution of occupations in the AEBFS between 1809 and 1850, presented in Table 2.4, shows the broad spectrum of society from which its members were drawn. Skilled workers, primarily craftsmen, formed the largest single occupational group, with 28 per cent of the total, although this was not quite as large as ser-

---

[3] References to members in the analysis of Tables 2.4 to 2.7 refer to new members. This is because information on occupations is available only for new members for most of the period.

vants/unskilled workers and labourers combined, with almost 30 per cent of the total. The trades/services occupational group was substantial at over 15 per cent and a tenth of the total were farmers. The smallest groupings were gentlemen i.e. those of independent means (7 per cent) and professionals (5.6 per cent).

Table 2.5 shows that, in the second half of the nineteenth century, the significance of different occupational groups had changed markedly.

Table 2.5

Occupational Categories of New Members 1850-99

Occupational Category	No. of Members	%
Gentleman	36	15.9
Professional	11	4.8
Farmer	25	11.0
Trades/Services	20	8.8
Skilled worker	45	19.8
Servant/Unskilled worker	38	16.7
Labourer	47	20.7
Miner	5	2.2
Total	227	99.9

Notes: See Table 2.4
Source: AEBFS, 2/1, 2/8, Books of Members, 1809-81, 1881-2000.

Labourers had become the single largest group and the combined servant/unskilled worker (16.7 per cent) and labourer groups (20.7 per cent) were now almost twice as large as the skilled worker group (19.8 per cent). The trades/services group had declined considerably in importance falling to only 8.8 per cent. The proportion of professionals remained low, at under 5 per cent, but the proportion of gentlemen had more than doubled to almost 16 per cent. As was also the case in the first half of the century, the high proportion of labourers, servants and other unskilled workers in membership is impressive as the quarterly subscription of 2s 6d or 3s would have represented a substantial outgoing relative to the low wage rates general at the time. It is clear from the Society's records, however, that whilst the very poorest members of society may not have been members, local labourers in steady employment were prepared to make the necessary financial sacrifice that membership entailed in order to insure themselves against pauperism. In addition, employers or farmers often paid (and still do) for their employees and/or sons to join.

The occupational profile changed again in the first half of the twentieth century (see Table 2.6). A major proportional increase was in the professional class, which more than doubled in significance and reflected a general expansion of the professions and of 'bureaucracy' from the late Victorian period through most of the twentieth century. Together with the gentleman group and the larger farmers, professionals would have comprised the majority of the Society's honorary members. Another striking change appears to have occurred in the proportion of farmers, which rose from 11 per cent in 1850-99 to 43 per cent in 1900-39. The large increases in the professional, trades/services (up from a little under 9 per cent to 16 per cent) and 'farmer' groups were offset by corresponding declines in the proportion of skilled workers, servants/unskilled workers and labourers.

Table 2.6

Occupational Categories of New Members 1900-39

Occupational Category	No. of Members	%
Gentleman	12	13
Professional	11	12
Farmer	40	43
Trades/Services	15	16
Skilled worker	10	11
Servant/Unskilled worker	3	3
Labourer	2	2
Miner	--	--
Total	93	100

Source: AEBFS, 2/8, Book of Members, 1881-2000.

The decrease in the proportion of labourers, falling from over 20 per cent to 2 per cent and servant/unskilled workers, falling from over 16 per cent to 3 per cent, may partly reflect changes in nomenclature but, with the introduction of the first state 'welfare' scheme in 1911, it is likely that many of the lower paid were content to look to the state for support in times of sickness and other adversity rather than seek membership of the AEBFS.

Table 2.7 shows that the occupational profile underwent a further shift in the middle years of the twentieth century. The proportion of gentlemen and professionals joining the Society dropping steeply, falling from a combined 25 per cent to a little over 11 per cent but this decline was offset by corresponding increases in the tradesmen/services and skilled worker groups. The proportion of labourers remained low and the farmer category was little changed at 39 per cent. Servants/other unskilled workers were no longer an identifiable group.

Table 2.7

Occupational Categories of New Members 1940-64[1]

Occupational Category	No. of Members	%
Gentleman	3	3.7
Professional	6	7.4
Farmer	32	39.4
Trades/Services	17	21.0
Skilled worker	17	21.0
Servant/Unskilled worker	--	--
Labourer	6	7.4
Miner	--	--
Total	81	99.9

[1] Unfortunately, from March 1964, after 160 years of detailed entries, the occupation of new members is rarely recorded. There are also occasional omissions immediately prior to 1964.
Source: see Table 2.6.

The changing proportions of new members in each of the occupational categories have to be treated with some caution. One factor affecting the occupational profile of the AEBFS, particularly from the late nineteenth century, was the decline of dual occupations. Many occupations, particularly crafts and mining were linked with farming. As these occupations declined people tended to move more fully into farming.

Askrigg Friendly Society members, 1929   Courtesy of *Northern Echo*

Moreover, while the different proportions are mainly the result of shifting occupational trends within the Society's membership and in the local community, some changes are probably due to changes in occupational designation. For example, in the nineteenth century some small farmers preferred to regard themselves as skilled-workers, for example, shepherds or foremen. However, in the twentieth century there was a stronger tendency to use the title of 'farmer'.

The consideration of occupations has so far concentrated on an analysis of new member occupations rather than on a profile of all members at any particular time. This is because of the manner in which the information is recorded (see footnote 3). Fortunately, however, comprehensive records do exist for one period, 1871 to 1875, and these allow a profile of occupations of all ordinary members to be constructed. Perhaps not unexpectedly, in 1871-5 there were no gentlemen and only one professional person – a school teacher – among the ordinary members. Contrary to the profile for the whole of the second part of the nineteenth century (see Table 2.5), there were only 8 farmers among the 103 occupations recorded in this period. Interestingly, although a wide range of occupations was recorded, many of the Society's ordinary members were in crafts (25) and trades (10); or were unspecified labourers (23). Perhaps surprisingly, only two live-in farm servants were recorded. Similarly, only two men, a hosier and a yarn spinner, worked in textiles. These men were probably employed at Low Mill, Askrigg, which was in the final years of its operation at this time. More surprisingly, given that the local lead and coal industries were virtually defunct by the 1870s, seven AEBFS members in the 1871-5 return were miners. Five of the miners were from two families: Michael (52 years) and John (47 years) Knowles lived in Woodhall, where there was still a little lead mining activity; and three others, John (40 years), George (38 years) and Edward (37 years) Tiplady, lived in Askrigg. William Brenkley (38 years) and Peter Thomson (35 years) lived in Sedbusk and Aysgarth respectively.[4]

Although it has not been possible since 1964 to identify occupations of new members, it is clear from discussions with existing members that, while farmers and tradesmen still feature strongly, many recent members, particularly honorary members, would have been termed 'gentleman' (i.e. living on their own means) or 'professional', in the nineteenth century. Currently, many of the members fall into these two categories while the 'Farmer' and 'Tradesmen' categories make up a high proportion of the remaining members.

---

4 Spellings of names varied in the AEBFS records and, often, from the version used today. The most frequently used spelling, found in the records, is used throughout this book.

Chapter 3

Articles of the Society

From the late eighteenth century, friendly societies became increasingly regulated by Acts of Parliament.[1] The legislation was designed primarily to ensure the financial viability of societies and to protect members from unscrupulous treasurers who, not infrequently, absconded with the funds. Members of Parliament and others hoped that the protection of the law would encourage the establishment of more friendly societies and that this, in turn, would reduce the burden on poor relief. Under the legislation, all societies who wished to receive the protection of the law were required to publish Articles (rules) of the society and register the society with the government office.[2] The AEBFS was keen to register as soon as possible after its formation. Its Articles were copied onto parchment by Society member, Clement Bell, a joiner, at a cost of £1 3s 6d, and were 'inrolled' [sic] with the local magistrate on 31 May, 1815. Unfortunately, the original parchment copy has been lost and the earliest extant copy of the Articles is the 1832 revision. The Society endeavoured not to amend the Articles too often but, inevitably, revisions were required from time to time. In addition to many supplementary rules, which were agreed over the years, full revisions of the Articles were published on the following dates:

Table 3.1

Revised Articles of the AEBFS

1832	1851	1876	1906	1918
1944	1953	1963	1969	1993

Source: AEBFS, 1/1-4, Articles of the Society and Supplementary Rules, 1832-1993.

---

1 The first Friendly Society Act was in 1793. Between that date and 1875 nineteen acts were passed.
2 Initially, registration was with local magistrates but from 1846 registration was formally taken over by the Registrar of Friendly Societies.

Although the Articles of the Society are known to have been revised on at least ten occasions, over the 190 years since its establishment in 1809, some elements remained constant. These included the strict entry requirements and the regulations covering both the condition and behaviour of members who submitted sickness claims for the payment of benefits.

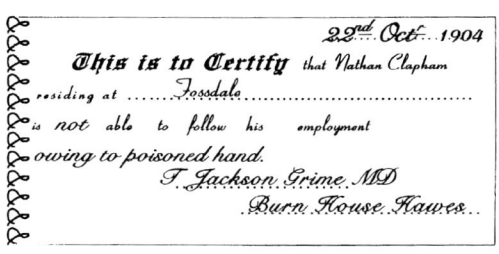

Certificate of Ill Health, 1904

The various editions of the Articles all followed a similar format. The aims and objectives were presented as part of the Introduction and, as the 1832 revision demonstrates, emphasised the value of the new Friendly Society to the 'lower orders' of society:

> as it gives them an opportunity…to lay up in store, against the time of necessity, a more ample provision than they could do individually for themselves.

The 1832 'Introduction' stressed the importance of 'peace and unanimity among ourselves' and stated that the major objective of the Society was to afford 'mutual pecuniary relief to its members, during sickness and helpless old age' (see Appendix 2).

Officers of the Society

The Officers of the Society (see Table 3.2) were important figures as their decisions, particularly those concerning payments and investments, could materially affect the viability of the Society. There are detailed descriptions in the Articles as to the roles and responsibilities of the Officers.

Table 3.2

Officers of the Society 1809-2000[1]

1809-50[2]	1851-2000
President	President
Vice President (permissory)	Vice President (1876)
Stewards (3)	Trustees (3)
Clerk	Stewards (3)
	Treasurer[3]
	Secretary

[1] Information taken from the various revisions of the Society's Articles.
[2] The only source of information on the Society's Officers available for this period is the 1832 Revised Articles. These Articles, and therefore the information they contain regarding the Society's Officers, are assumed to have remained current until the next known revision of the Articles in 1851. It is also assumed, in the absence of contrary information, that the Society's Officers were the same for the period 1809-31 as for 1832.
[3] Formerly designated Clerk.
Source: AEBFS, 3/5/1, Cash and Minute Book, 1809-81; 2/7, Minute Book, 1881-present.

In addition to its Officers, the AEBFS, from 1851, had a Committee of Management, consisting of nine members.[3] While the Trustees and Secretary were permanent appointments, the President, Treasurer, two Stewards and eight members of the Committee were appointed annually. Although, in 1832 the clerk was paid an annual salary of 10s, from 1851 no officers were paid salaries. The Articles provided that no-one who had been President could be re-elected within two years. However, it appears that this rule was not strictly adhered to (see Appendix 3). The 1851 Articles deemed that, if practicable, the Committee should consist of at least three honorary members and five ordinary members. This was modified, in 1876, to four honorary and five ordinary members. Further, all Management Committee appointments were to be for one year only, though members could be re-appointed. In the same year the Articles noted that the President, if possible, should be

---

3 The 1832 Articles allowed for an ad hoc Committee of nine members to be formed when necessary to resolve a specific issue.

an honorary member and that one of the Stewards should also be the Treasurer. This structure has remained largely unchanged to the present day.

Askrigg Friendly Society members, 1953   Courtesy of H. Trotter

The Officers of the AEBFS, and particularly the Management Committee, were, and still are, responsible for ensuring the efficient running and financial viability of the Society. Some Officers served for many years. For example, Tom Bowling retired in 1988 after being secretary for 21 years. However, his length of service was exceeded by Alexander T. Storey, who joined the Society in 1863 as a 20-year old labourer and who was the Secretary for 49 years from 1887 to 1936.

Rules of the AEBFS

Life in the nineteenth century was hard for many people and occupations were often hazardous. As friendly societies throughout the country were concerned to protect themselves from too many calls on their precious funds, exclusion clauses covering certain dangerous occupations were often inserted in the Articles. However, reflecting the importance of mining in the area in the nineteenth century, the AEBFS took a more liberal view and, apart from the military and seafarers, no occupation was excluded. Fortunately, the Society was not inundated by applications from miners; in fact, in the whole 190 years of its existence, only 12 miners and 2 colliers joined.

Although the AEBFS was more liberal than many societies concerning occupations, it did take a strong moral stance. The Articles stated that no one who was 'of notoriously scandalous life or conversation' would be admitted to the Society. This restriction lasted for 160 years until 1969 when, perhaps in keeping with the greater permissiveness of the times, the rule was removed. Despite the generally strict moral tenor of the Society's rules, individuals born out of wedlock were not barred from membership. For example, the Society's records show that Thomas Bushby and Ralph Harker, who were elected to membership of the Society in 1856 and 1859 respectively, were both born out of wedlock.[4]

It was a frequent requirement of friendly societies that their members should be in work and the rules of many societies included provision for payment of an allowance to enable members to travel in search of work. Perhaps surprisingly, given the relatively large-scale out-migration from the area, the Askrigg Society did not offer this allowance.

In the nineteenth century, a man wanting to join the Society had to inform the Steward and attend a meeting to 'notify publically [sic] such a desire' and then withdraw while a vote was taken. However, by the late twentieth century this rule had been modified. In 1969 the requirement was simply that any aspiring member must be proposed and seconded by an existing member. In the early years of the Society prospective members had to confirm that they were in good health but in 1876 the rule was changed and before admittance a doctor had to certify that the applicant was of sound constitution and in a fit state of health. Some of the medical certificates survive from the late nineteenth century. Originally medical certificates were hand-written but from the 1890s specially printed certification forms were used.

---

4 Interestingly, the baptismal certificates provide an indication of levels of literacy in Wensleydale. Formal education was not available to many people in the early nineteenth century and as late as the 1860s some of the parents in Wensleydale were still signing their name on the baptism form with an X.

> December 2nd 1899
>
> **This is to Certify** that I have examined
> ......James Trotter..........................
> and find him in a fit state of health to be
> admitted into the ....Askrigg..............
> Club.
>
> (Signed) Alfred Baker.
> James Kitcher....

Doctor's Certificate of Fitness, 1899

Although the Articles specified the procedure for the admittance of new members to the Society, they do not reflect the level of paperwork required. It was important to ensure that new applicants were telling the truth about their age, so from the earliest days prospective members were required to show their baptismal (later birth) certificate. If the original certificate was lost or there was a later query concerning the age of an individual (particularly in respect of eligibility for the 70-year old benefit), the 'birthplace' vicar was requested to write and verify the facts.

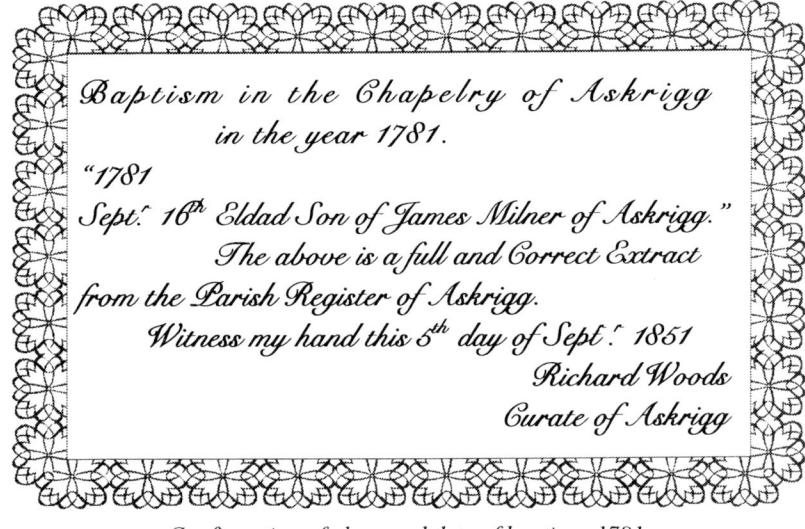

> Baptism in the Chapelry of Askrigg
> in the year 1781.
> "1781
> Sept.r 16th Eldad Son of James Milner of Askrigg."
> The above is a full and Correct Extract
> from the Parish Register of Askrigg.
> Witness my hand this 5th day of Sept.r 1851
> Richard Woods
> Curate of Askrigg

Confirmation of place and date of baptism, 1781

Admission to the AEBFS of men who were not born in Askrigg frequently caused difficulties. It is clear that men from other parts of Wensleydale were eager to join the Society. For example, of the 305 members who joined the Society between 1809 and 1859, little more than half (163) were recorded as living in Askrigg. Nearly all the other members lived elsewhere in Wensleydale. However, some were born or baptised further afield and this caused additional complications. For example, William Coates Metcalfe was born in Askrigg on 1 August 1843 but was baptised at the Congregational Chapel, Low Row, Swaledale on 31 August 1843. The Congregational Minister was required to confirm this to the Society in writing. In 1852 Parkin Blades, a servant at 'Field House' near Bainbridge, applied to join the Society. Parkin had been born in Mallerstang, Westmorland and the Vicar of Mallerstang was asked to provide written confirmation that Parkin had been born on April 17, 1829. The opening of the Wensleydale railway in 1878 exacerbated the problems relating to birthplace. George Potter, a railway guard living in Askrigg, applied to join the Society in 1880. George had been born at Forncett in Norfolk on 4 June 1851 and was required to obtain a copy of his birth certificate from the Registrar in Depwade, Norfolk. He was successful and was admitted into the Society on 2 June 1881. Although the early rule books placed no distance restriction on new members, the 1874 revision stipulated that ordinary members had to live within 15 miles of Askrigg, a change which was perhaps made in anticipation of the imminent arrival of the railway.

I hereby certify that James the Son of George & Elizabeth Milner, Stone Mason of Thornton Rust in the Parish of Aysgarth, was baptized Decr 8^d 1826 by me.

John Winn
Vicar of Aysgarth
Decr 8^d 1852.

Confirmation of place and date of baptism, 1826

Askrigg Friendly Society members, 1960 Courtesy of H. Trotter
(for details see p.102)

According to the Articles, members who joined the AEBFS and subsequently left the area were able to continue as members but were subject to certain restrictions when claiming benefits. Richard Trotter, an Askrigg corn dealer, joined in 1856 but continued as a member when he left the village to become a policeman in Liverpool. Likewise, William Lambert, a labourer from Greensley Bank, joined in 1872. Sometime later he moved to find work in Shildon, Durham but continued to pay his AEBFS subscriptions.

Although, the early rule books precluded members living abroad from claiming benefits, this restriction was omitted from the 1876 rules. Shortly afterwards, this relaxation caused a problem. One member, Ezra Heseltine, who had joined the Society in 1864 when he was a labourer, had subsequently emigrated.[5] In October 1880 he wrote to the Society to ask for sick relief. This threw the Management Committee into a quandary. Heseltine had regularly paid his subscriptions to the Society but the Committee had no way of ascertaining whether he, or any other similar claimants, were telling the truth. In the end it was decided to repay all Heseltine's subscriptions and to reinstate the rule that emigrants could not claim benefits from the Society.

---

5 Heseltine's destination is not recorded.

> 2nd March 1900
>
> This is to Certify that I have examined ....James Daykin.... and find him in a fit state of health to be admitted into the ......Askrigg...... Club.
>
> (Signed) Alfred Baker
> M.R.C.S.E.

Doctor's Certificate of Fitness, 1900

One of the main purposes of the rules was to protect against fraudulent claims and to safeguard the good name of the Society. Once an applicant had been accepted into membership of the Society, he was required to observe its rules. The rules sometimes extended into unexpected areas. For example, in 1851 it was stipulated that any member convicted of poaching was to be fined one guinea in the first instance and was to be expelled from the Society for a repeat offence. These penalties were still in force in 1969 though by 1993 they had been removed from the rule book.

Active interest in the Society was a serious matter and attendance at meetings was compulsory, with fines imposed on absentees. Decorum at meetings was considered important and in May 1820 a supplementary rule was introduced stating that any member wearing his hat in the Club Room would be fined 6d. In order to ensure 'decency and regularity' at meetings, fines were imposed for a variety of other offences including swearing, gaming, 'causing debate concerning Church and State', and seditious speaking. The latter offence was considered to be extremely serious particularly in the early part of the nineteenth century. In 1830 there had been many disturbances across England by farm workers and country people. In particular, the 'Captain Swing' riots, which occurred mainly in East Anglia, caused much concern among the authorities. Likewise, in 1834, the 'Tolpuddle Martyrs' were accused and found guilty of taking a seditious oath at their trade union meeting at the village pub in Tolpuddle, Dorset. The Tolpuddle group comprised mainly local trades and craftsmen, farmers and labourers and several of those convicted were transported to Australia. The Askrigg Society was keen to show that it was not a subversive union or a political society. By having strict rules it sought to ensure that its members behaved in a law-abiding manner. The list of offences and fines relating to political and religious discussions and seditious behaviour, remained in the Society's rules until the 1990s.

		S.	D.
1.	Cursing and Swearing in the Society's Room, each offence	1	0
2.	Using Abusive Language in the Society's Room	1	0
3.	Upbraiding any Member for receiving Sick Allowance, even out of the Society's Room	1	0
4.	Ditto, second offence	2	6
5.	Ditto, third or any subsequent offence (or if thought proper by a majority of Members, expulsion)	5	0
6.	Smoking in the Society's Room before allowed by the President	1	0
7.	Quarrelling or Fighting in the Society's Room	2	0
8.	Refusing to be seated when called to order by any Officer in the Society's Room	1	0
9.	A second offence of Refusal	2	0
10.	Causing Debates concerning Church or State	1	0
11.	Appearing in Liquor in the Society's Room	1	0
12.	Molesting or using Abusive Language to the President, Secretary, Stewards, or other Officer of the Society in the discharge of their duty	2	6
13.	Not attending the Service in the Church at the Annual Meeting.	1	0
14.	Speaking seditiously in the Society's Room	5	0
15.	Occasioning Quarrels or Disturbances within the Town of Askrigg on the day of the Annual Meeting	1	0
16.	Any Member convicted of treasonable Conspiracies shall be excluded.		

Fines for breaking Society meeting rules (taken from 1969 Articles)

Obviously, the Society's main outgoings were for sickness and death benefit and the strict rules governing these are discussed in Chapter 5. However, the Society also rewarded good health and, from the earliest days, the rules stated that members attaining the age of 70 years would receive a bonus as long as they had not made sustained claims on the Society for sickness benefits. Given the age profile of the Society in the early years, it is perhaps not surprising that by 1850 only seven members had claimed their £5 bonus for achieving the age of 70 years, though, as shown in Chapter 4, there were more claims in later years.

The Articles of the AEBFS have served the purpose of ensuring that, not only was the Society carefully organised, but payment of benefits was strictly regulated and fair. This helped to ensure that the Society's funds were efficiently used for its deserving members with legitimate claims.

Askrigg Friendly Society members, 1969   Courtesy of T.E. Metcalfe

Row 1: D. Sharpe, A. Kirkbride, J.T. Peacock, M. Scarr, B. Horner, (J. Trotter), R. Lambert, M. Weatherald, T. Metcalfe, R. Daykin, J. Thompson, J. Peacock Snr., (L. Scarr), B. Kirkbride, H. Cockerill, D. Scarr Snr., R. Brass, G. Siddle. *Row 2*: J. Harrison, A. Chapman, B. Ponsonby, J. Halton, J.J. Sunter, D. Middleton, W. Dinsdale, M. Bell, S. Peacock, F. Lambert, J. Holdsworth, W. Preston, Rev. M. Stonestreet, R. Balderstone. *Row 3*: J. Scarr Snr., E. Burton, J. Abraham, H. Trotter, T. Bowling, J. Hemsley, P. Metcalfe, C. Cunningham, J.C.P. Ellwood, J. Gregson, T. Kirkbride, B. Banks, D. Abraham, F. Percival, C. Gaskell. *Row 4*: E.J. Adamson, K. Slack, I. Tallantire, Dr. J.B. Coltman, A. Scarr, D. Chapman, M.Scott Snr., P.E. Hartley, T. Scott, R. Scott, R.E. Dale, N.K. Sumter, C. Grainger, J. Piper, L. Vincent. *Row 5*: S. Cockerill, J. Scarr Jnr., S. Hodgson, D. Daykin, D. Metcalfe, D. Widdows, S. Bell, W.J. Metcalfe, L. Alderson, K. Wetherill, J. Fawcett, W. Balderstone, R. Hopper, W. Metcalfe. *Row 6*: B. Bell, S. Bell, R. Trotter, G. Percival, R. Middleton, R. Fawcett, R. Scarr, D. Scarr Jnr., J.R. Lambert, H. Gregson, J. Fawcett, S. Bell.

29

Chapter 4

The Finances of the Society

Subscriptions

Without adequate funds friendly societies could not survive. Subscriptions paid by members were, therefore, vitally important if a society was to meet its commitments and prosper.

Table 4.1 shows that AEBFS subscriptions, although changing over the 190 years, frequently remained at the same level for long periods.

Table 4.1

Changes in Quarterly Subscriptions 1809-2000

Year	Subscription
1809	3s 0d
1833	2s 6d
1876	3s 0d
c1900	4s 0d
1904	3s 8d - 5s 7d[1]
1904	9s 2½d - 13s 9s[2]
c1965	5s 8d[3]
c1965	11s 2½d[4]
1969	7s 2d[3]
1969	17s 3d[4]
2000	£2 10s[5]

[1] Contribution range for a 16 year old at entry depending upon scale of benefits chosen – see Table 4.2.
[2] Contribution range for a 45 year old at entry – see Table 4.2.
[3] Contribution of a 16 year old at entry.
[4] Contribution of a 45 year old at entry.
[5] £2 10s in old pence = £2.50 new pence. At this date honorary members paid an annual subscription of £3.

Source: See Tables 3.1-2 and AEBFS, 3/5/2, Cash Book, 1881-1941.

In 1809 members of the Society decided that initially the quarterly subscription would be 3s but once funds had reached £500 the rate would be reduced to 2s 6d per quarter. Partly as a result of sickness and death benefits being paid out from 1811, the funds took time to build up and the target of £500 was not reached for nearly 20 years. Eventually, in 1833, subscriptions were reduced from 3s to 2s 6d. Due to a high level of membership and judicious investment, the Society's funds remained in a very healthy state and there was no increase in subscriptions for over forty years. In 1876 the subscription was increased to its former level of 3s and remained at this level until the beginning of the twentieth century. However, during this period the Society's funds slowly declined and, by the turn of the century, were in a serious state.

The 1875 Friendly Societies Act required the submission of quinquennial returns to the Registrar of Friendly Societies. Extant Returns for the AEBFS date from 1890 and several include reports from Mr Farnworth, the Society's actuary/accountant. The comments were generally favourable in respect of the Society's vitality but often included suggestions concerning subscriptions. For example, Mr Farnworth congratulated the Society in 1890 for turning the deficit of 1886 into a surplus (see Appendix 4). He noted that this turn-round was largely due to actual claims for sickness and death benefit consistently being lower than expected on the basis of actuarial tables. However, Mr Farnworth voiced concern about the age profile of members in 1890 and noted that the existing structure of subscriptions required modification. He suggested that more young people would be attracted to the Society if a graduated rate of contribution was introduced. While he accepted that the standard entry subscription was partly offset by a low maximum entry age of 30 years, he maintained that a graduated rate would allow younger people to pay less on entry than an older person. The Society, hoping that the age profile would improve without altering the existing subscription system, decided not to act on the advice. Unfortunately, the situation grew steadily worse.

In 1900 Mr Farnworth issued a dire warning noting that, based on number and age of members, "the Society is gradually but surely decaying". He urged yet again that, although the AEBFS was "liberally supported by donations", a graduated scale of subscriptions should be introduced. In 1904 Farnworth gravely declared, "It is my duty to direct your attention to…a serious deficit", and he strongly advised prompt action. This time the Committee took his warnings to heart and introduced both a graded entry and four scales of contribution. As Table 4.2 demonstrates, the higher the subscription paid the greater the benefits. The four scales enabled new members to choose one which best suited their needs or their purse.

Table 4.2

Selected Premiums and Benefits 1904

Age at Entry	Scale 1	Scale 4
16 years	3s 8d	5s 7d
45 years	9s 2d	13s 9d

Benefits		
for first 4 wks	10s 6d	for first 6 mths 12s 0d
next 22 wks	7s 0d	---
rest of sickness	5s 0d	6s 0d
death of member	£4 0s 0d	£12 0s 0d
death of member's wife	£3 0s 0d	£6 0s 0d
on reaching 70 years*	£5 0s 0d	£5 0s 0d

* providing the member has not claimed more than £30 benefit from the Society during the period of his membership.
Source: AEBFS, 1/1/4, Articles of the AEBFS, 1904.

The 1904 graduated scale should have been more attractive to young low-paid workers as, although annual subscriptions to the Society had risen by 47 per cent from the mid-1830s to 1904, an agricultural labourer's pay had risen on average from 11s 4d to 18s 3d per week, a rise of 61 per cent.[1] This suggests that by the early twentieth century it had become easier for the poorer inhabitants of Wensleydale to join the AEBFS. However, the move to a graduated system failed in its objec-

---

1   The 47 per cent rise is derived from the mid-1830s subscription of 10s per annum and a 16-year old Scale 1 subscription in 1904 of 14s 8d. Labourer's pay taken from A.L. Bowley, *Wages in the UK in the nineteenth century*, 1898 and A. Wilson Fox, 'Agricultural wages in England and Wales during the last fifty years', *JRSS*, LXVI, 1903.

tive, at least in the short term, because as was shown earlier, compared with the first part of the nineteenth century, fewer unskilled working men were joining the Society in the early 1900s.

The lack of a good response from young local men was possibly also influenced by the fact that the Society, although retaining the graded age-at-entry subscriptions, by 1906 had dropped the graded scale of benefits. Perhaps also, the graduated system was too complicated for a relatively small society to operate successfully. Despite these problems, the graded subscription rates continued and by 1969 the quarterly rates were 7s 2d for a 16-year old and 17s 3d for a 45-year old man. Eventually the graded subscriptions issue came full circle and, in 1993, a single quarterly subscription rate of £2.50 (£2 10s) was reintroduced.

Extract from the Subscription Book, 1859-60

Askrigg Friendly Society members, 1985   Snowden Mason
(for details see p.102)

Entry Fees

In addition to subscriptions, new members were required to pay an entry, or proposal, fee and were expected to purchase a copy of the Society's Articles. Although the initial entry fee of the AEBFS was 2s 6d, this was soon reduced to 6d. This was very low when compared with most other friendly societies whose entry fees ranged from 5s to £2. The Askrigg Society kept its fees as low as possible because, as part of an independent and relatively isolated community, it wished to encourage as many as possible of the poorly paid workers in regular employment to join. However, while maintaining the low entry fee principle, the Society had to abandon the 6d level by the mid-nineteenth century and raise the entrance fee once again to 2s 6d, a level which was maintained for most of the twentieth century. In 1993 an entry fee of £1 was charged but by 1996 the entry fee had been finally abandoned.

AEBFS payment of subscriptions, c1985   Courtesy of H. Trotter

Fines - Missed Payments

The flow of funds was the lifeblood of the Society and unexpected dips in income could be serious. It was important, therefore, that penalties were imposed on members who missed payment of subscriptions. In the early nineteenth century, a fine of 6d was levied for missed payments and all non-payers were excluded from the quarterly meeting. However, it appears that these rules were not always strictly enforced and, apparently, mitigating circumstances were taken into account. For example, although William Banks, a carrier from Askrigg, missed two payments in 1822, no fines were recorded and he eventually made good the short-fall in contributions.

Not surprisingly it was the poorer people who were under greatest pressure in keeping up their subscriptions. In the first part of the nineteenth century servants and unskilled workers were most likely to miss payments, but tradesmen and agricultural labourers were also frequent offenders. Perhaps the tradesmen were less reliable because of unexpected fluctuations in their incomes – or perhaps because late payments were an occupational hazard!

Arrears of subscriptions have been a problem throughout the life of the Society and fines continue to be imposed. However, in the twentieth century as AEBFS benefits became less important in the light of state support, more members fell into arrears. The 'loss' to the Society could be significant. For example, in 1996 the cumulative arrears from 53 members amounted to £727.66.

Actuaries and Accountants

From its inception the AEBFS had kept careful accounts of its income and expenditure. After the 1850 Friendly Societies Act, the Society was required to submit its rules and accounts to the Registrar of Friendly Societies. By the late nineteenth century, as a result of a requirement in the 1875 Friendly Societies Act, the AEBFS employed an accountant, who was also an actuary, to prepare the increasingly complex accounts, returns and quinquennial valuations. Mr Farnworth was well equipped to act as actuary and to audit the Society's accounts. He was based in Preston, Lancashire and was consulting actuary to many friendly societies including the:

> United Ancient Order of Druids' (800 Lodges)
> British Order of Ancient Free Gardeners (400 Lodges)
> Royal Hearts of Oak Yearly Dividing Friendly Society (300,000 Lodges)

Mr Farnworth continued to act for the Society until 1924. After this date the roles of accountant and actuary were split and the Askrigg Management Committee decided to employ W.A. Curtis, a London actuary, to prepare the 1931 quinquennial returns. From 1939 the AEBFS employed a different actuary, C. Rattray of Reigate and, ten years later, Mr Lane of London took over as the Society's actuary. His firm Lane, Clark and Peacock undertook the quinquennial valuations up to 1989 after which date the Society was no longer required to submit valuations. During the period 1936-54, the Annual Returns were prepared by a Newcastle accountancy firm, J.C. Graham and Spoor. This firm became Henson and Spoor and continued to audit the Society's Returns until 1976 when G. McCowrie of Newcastle took over as the Society's accountant. His firm McCowrie, Ramshaw & Co. have continued to fulfil this role to the present day.

The Funds of the Society

In March 1809, the AEBFS started life with funds of £7 10s, which had been carried forward from the defunct Wensleydale Union Society. The subscriptions and donations of the first members quickly increased this to £25 in 1810 and to approximately £271 in 1820. As membership continued to grow and more money came into the Society, capital quickly accrued and was invested in the form of private loans on interest. By 1859 the total funds of the Society had risen to £1,259 and by 1867 stood at £1,613. As Table 4.3 shows, although there were some significant reverses, even allowing for inflation the funds of the Society have grown significantly over the last 190 years.

Table 4.3

Total Funds of AEBFS, 1810-1999[1]

	£		£
1810	25	1924	1133
1820	271[2]	1931	1185
1830	472	1939	1398
1840	849	1949	1803
1850	1140	1959	2840
1860	1359	1969	5971
1870	1676	1979	8814
1880	2040	1989	15,168
1890	2783	1993	19,704
1900	2910	1999	22,799

[1] As at June [4th quarter] each year to nearest £.
[2] Approximate figure.
Note:
1 The figures from 1890 onwards are taken from the quinquennial or annual returns.
2 Some records are missing and totals may vary slightly from other extant totals.
3 The figures above are at current prices (i.e. not present day prices). Account must be taken of inflation which was very low in the nineteenth century but was very high in periods of the twentieth century.
Source: AEBFS, 3/1, Annual Returns; 3/5/1-2, Cash Books; 3/6, Quinquennial Valuations; 1809-1999.

One of the major problems for all friendly societies was protection of funds. Although, fortunately, the Askrigg Society has never had any problems of fraud, nevertheless it took great care to protect its funds. Initially all monies were kept in an iron chest, known as 'the box', which was held at the King's Arms Inn. The chest had three locks and, to ensure security, the President, the Steward and the publican each held a key. By 1824 surplus funds were rapidly accruing and in September of that year £110 was placed in a deposit account at the nearest local bank, the Savings Bank in Leyburn. Thereafter, sums were deposited regularly. For example, £90 was paid in during the quarter ending 6 June 1827 and a further £137 was deposited for the quarter ending 4 June 1828. The box at the King's Arms was still used to hold some cash because easily accessible funds were required so that benefits could speedily be disbursed to needy members. In 1836 the Savings Bank in Leyburn became the Swaledale and Wensleydale Banking Company. When the Company opened a branch in nearby Hawes in 1842, the Society saved itself the 13 mile journey to Leyburn and transferred its account to Hawes. The Swaledale and Wensleydale Bank was taken over by Barclays Bank in the early twentieth century and the Society's current and deposit accounts continue to be with Barclays Bank in Hawes. The system whereby the Society's surplus monies have been periodically invested has applied throughout its existence and remains essentially unchanged to the present day.

The assets of the Society accrued from three sources: subscriptions, donations and interest on loans or other investments. For most of the nineteenth century the 'running costs' of the Society and the payment of benefits were drawn from current monies and not capital. In fact, although the actual amount fluctuated, there was usually a modest surplus from the current funds. For example, in June 1842 the surplus from subscriptions, donations and interest over the previous year was £41 8s 9d and in June 1877 there was a surplus of £19 8s 9d.

Due to the lack of official valuations, it is difficult to gain a precise picture of the state of the Society's finances for most of the nineteenth century. However, from 1890, when the quinquennial valuations became available, a clearer picture begins to emerge (see Table 4.4). Judicious loans and investments had ensured that the Society's funds were in a healthy state for most of the nineteenth century. However, by the turn of the twentieth century, when there was a quinquennial deficit of £318 and the AEBFS was worth only 17s 10d in the £ (as opposed to 19s 1d in the £ in 1895), the Society, as Mr Farnworth had observed, was in serious trouble. Mr Farnworth considered that, in order to improve membership, adult female members should be admitted and, as allowed under the terms of the 1896 Friendly Societies Act, the Society should also consider admitting juniors. Although the Society adopted some of Mr Farnworth's other ideas, it decided not to take up these two suggestions.

Table 4.4

Funds of the AEBFS, 1890-1989[1]

	Total value £	Surplus £	Deficit £	Solvency Rate	No. of Members	VBM[2]
1890	2,783	116			104	27
1900	2,910		318	17s 10d	97	30
1910[3]	--					
1924[4]	1,133		300	14s 8d[5]	48	24
1929	868	105			46	19
1939	1,398	542		32s 8d	51	27
1949	1,908	105		21s 2d	43	44
1959	2,904	64		20s 5d	81	36
1969	5,971		653	17s 9d	115	74
1979	8,814	3,692		34s 5d	122	72
1989	15,223	9,238		36s	129	118

[1] At current prices i.e. not present day prices; 1989 was the final Quinquennial Valuation submitted by the Society.
[2] Value per Benefit Member
[3] 1910 Quinquennial Valuation is missing as are the 1905 and 1915 Valuations.
[4] 1919 Quinquennial Valuation is missing.
[5] Not noted
Note: Some records are missing and totals may vary slightly from other extant totals.
Source: See Table 4.3.

Despite some action being undertaken in respect of subscriptions and investments in 1904, the financial position of the Society continued to worsen. By 1919 the quinquennial deficit had increased to £487 and the Society had a 'solvency rate' of only 12s 4d in the £.[2] However, the introduction of graduated subscriptions and changes in investment policy eventually paid off and a slow recovery ensued. Although, in 1924, the Society still had a deficit of £300, the 'solvency rate' had improved to 14s 8d in the £. Mr Farnworth noted that the

---

2 The 1919 deficit and solvency rate was noted in the 1924 valuation.

financial situation was still greatly aided by light sickness costs and a low rate of mortality in Wensleydale but again, in order to place the Society on a more secure footing, he urged the use of "sound and attractive tables of contributions and benefits". The slow recovery continued. However, in 1969 there was another quinquennial deficit. This time the main causes were increasing professional and registration fees; increases in sickness benefits; and more stringent valuations which had been adopted as a result of the recent trend in claims. Once again, the Society took necessary action and survived the crisis. By 1984 a healthy quinquennial surplus of £4,770 had accrued.

Statement of the Society Funds

	£	s	d		£	s	d
Amount invested on North Eastern Railways Co. Debenture	1500	0	0	Payments brought forward	59	8	8
D⁰ on Swaledale & Wensleydale Banking Corp. Deposit Receipt with Int. up to 1st June instant	100	1	6	Paid Matthew Metcalfe of Bradford for 13 days sick allowance from the 18th to the 30th of March	-	12	-
Amount of balance in the Box as shown above	13	4	8	D⁰. to William Banks for 10 days from the 15th to 26th April	-	10	-
Total amount of Society's funds this day	£1613	6	2	D⁰. William Banks's funeral allowance	2	10	-
				D⁰. for Postage Stamps and Envelopes	-	1	8
Amount of Society's funds last Annual Meeting	£1588	9	5				
Net amount of gain to the Society's funds in the Year	£24	16	9	D⁰. Minister's fee for Sermon	-	10	-
				D⁰. William Pratt bonus on attaining 70 years of age	5	-	-
					68	11	11
				Paid years rent on the Club Room	5	-	-
				Club Room Annual Meeting 6th June 1867	73	11	11

I have examined the accounts and approve of and allow the same on behalf of the Society

John Chapman
pro: President

Example of a Statement of AEBFS Funds, June 1867

Investments

The Management Committee is responsible for ensuring that subscription and donation income is invested in the most effective manner. Originally, investments were in the form of private interest-bearing loans to local people with sufficient collateral. The earliest reference to one of these loans was in 1809 when J. Dinsdale & Co. received £15 on interest.[3] In December of the same year, James Weatherald & Co. received £20 on interest. As the Society needed to retain only a small floating fund for payment of benefits and other costs, more and more loans were given as the Society's capital grew. By 1820, £270 19s 4d of the Society's funds was in the form of loans and, in the same year, £45 16s 3d was received in interest.[4] In 1829 the treasurer noted that £300 was deposited 'on mortgage'.

By the 1840s substantial funds were invested as private loans. For example, Ernest Simpson, possibly of Aysgarth, had a loan of £400, and Swaledale farmer, Richard Guy and his nephew, George, of Usha Gate (Gap) near Thwaite, each had a loan of £200 at a rate of 4½ per cent interest. By 1856, £1,250 of the Society's funds was in 'several joint bonds'.

In the 1860s another investment opportunity attracted the Society's Management Committee. From the beginning of the Victorian era railway building had caught the imagination of the country and 1860 saw the beginning of a second national railway construction boom. Since the 1840s local dalespeople had hoped that a railway would be built through Wensleydale. This became even more likely from the 1860s when, after a series of proposals, the North Eastern Railway Company put forward a feasible plan which resulted in an Act being passed in 1870. It took several years for the local railway, which had a station at Askrigg, to be constructed and the line was not fully opened until 1878.

Possibly as a result of the interest generated by the likelihood of a railway being constructed in Wensleydale, the Trustees and Stewards were convinced that railways would be a sound investment for the Society's funds and on 24 April 1861 convened a meeting of the Management Committee in order to put forward their ideas. There was

---

3 Unfortunately, the rate of interest is not given for many of the loans.
4 The interest figure is likely to have been an accumulated figure rather than an annual figure.

clearly much debate about the proposed radical change in the Society's investment policy but finally it was agreed that a total of £1,400 be invested in 'NER Co. Mortgage Debenture'. This sum was raised by calling in all existing loans and receiving a loan of £26 17s 6d 'to make up an even sum' from the Askrigg solicitor, Mr George Winn, who was an honorary member of the Management Committee. By 1867 the Society's investment in the NER had been increased to a total of £1,500.

> Club Room 24th April 1861 – at a meeting of the Committee of Management of this society club, convened by the stewards and justified for the purpose of determining the best mode of investing the funds of the society, and instructing the Trustees thereon
>
> Matthew Willis MD in the chair
>
> It was unanimously resolved and determined that the Trustees of the Society be requested to invest the sum of £600 now available for that purpose on security of the North Eastern Railway Company's Mortgage Debenture in their own names at the best rate of interest they can obtain.
>
> The Revd Richard Wood and Mr George Winn, the Trustees of the Society having a sum of £800 invested in their joint names on the like Security of the North Eastern Railway Company's Mortgage Debenture at 4 ¼ per cent. It was unanimously resolved and determined by this meeting that the investment and security of the said sum of £800 be and is hereby accepted by and on behalf of the Society as part of the Monies and Funds of the said Society, the same to continue as now in the joint names of the said Richard Wood and George Winn in Trust for the Society –
> As witness our hands -
>
> Matthew Willis MD
> Chairman
> Geo Winn   Geo Bell
> Geo Coates   Matthew Metcalfe

AEBFS Minutes re railway investment

The Society held railway stocks until 1881 when there was another change in investment policy. This time the Management Committee resolved to invest in land. The decision was probably taken as the result of rising land prices in the 1860s and 1870s, when farming enjoyed a period of prosperity. Unfortunately, the late 1870s saw the

43

onset of an agricultural depression which was to last for nearly 20 years. However, the Society was not to know there would be such a prolonged period of difficulty in farming. In March 1881, the Committee paid £1,710 to purchase the 53-acre Shaw Farm at Lunds. Honorary member, William Winn, who had succeeded his father as solicitor, acted for the Society regarding the purchase and charged £26 10s 2d for his services.

The foray into real estate was not a very happy experience for the AEBFS. Throughout the Society's ownership of the farm, there were problems of a kind that beset many landlords. These included maintenance of the estate, the difficulty of finding suitable tenants and receiving prompt payment of rent. In 1883, the Society replaced the farm's chimney at a cost of 13s. In August 1885, Mr Wilmot, the agent of Lord Wharncliffe, demanded £26 8s from the Society for payment of arrears of the Lord's Rent due from the farm. Lord Wharncliffe was quite keen to terminate this relatively small annual income and so Wilmot suggested that the Society could purchase the Lord's Rent and settle the arrears for a total of £100. The Society speedily agreed to this suggestion.

By 1891 the tenant, Jeffrey Metcalfe, was in arrears with his rent and was considering leaving the farm. The Society was obviously concerned at the prospect of losing a good tenant and having the farm 'on hand'. In order to try to keep Metcalfe, Committee members decided that if he took the farm at £38 per annum from 6 April 1892 and agreed to continue occupying the farmhouse and keep up fencing, the Society would write off his arrears. However, if Metcalfe decided to leave, the Society would require him to pay the outstanding rent arrears. At first it appeared that Metcalfe had agreed to the proposed terms and notified the Society that he was in the process of buying and erecting wire fencing. However, something caused Metcalfe to change his mind and, in November 1891, the Society moved quickly and demanded all the outstanding rent. At the same time the Society actively sought a new tenant. Posters were distributed inviting tenders for the farm which was to be let on an annual tenancy. The conflict rumbled on and the disgruntled Metcalfe countered the demand letter with a request that he be allowed to offset his arrears against fencing and other work he claimed to have undertaken on behalf of his AEBFS landlord. Eventually, in order to resolve the issue, the Management

Committee reluctantly agreed to allow him £11 10s 6d for the work he claimed to have undertaken.

It was with some relief that, shortly afterwards, the Society received an offer from John Atkinson of Nateby in Westmorland to rent Shaw Farm for £35 per annum for 10 years, and to build a stone wall for 8s 6d a rood. The Management Committee felt that, given the uncertainty of the times, they could not be tied to the same rent for 10 years. However, they were concerned that whoever took the farm should also occupy it and not farm it from a distance. So Atkinson was offered a package whereby the Society agreed to maintain the rent at £35 per annum for at least 3 years but that the new tenant must occupy the farm. The Society also accepted Atkinson's price to build the 5ft 6ins high stone wall and the deal was struck. However, the investment was still not providing a good return and maintenance costs continued to be an additional drain. In 1892, the Society partly offset the £25 10s owing to Atkinson for walling against his half year's rent of £17 10s. The Society also had to provide a new grate and oven at a cost of £1 9s 9d. Further, in 1895, Atkinson complained that the barn was in a bad state and asked for repairs to be undertaken. A visit to the barn by two Committee members, Bland Spence, a slater, and Thomas Weatherald, a builder, confirmed that the barn needed re-roofing. Tenders for the repair work were invited from local workmen in the Hawes area but none were received. The Committee, therefore, agreed that the tender of £13 15s 6d from Thomas Weatherald be accepted.

By 1895 the Society's investment in real estate was causing great concern to Mr Farnworth. On the one hand, the farm was giving a very poor rate of return and, on the other hand, Farnworth felt that the investment was not really compatible with Friendly Society regulations. By 1900 the situation had worsened and Farnworth urged that action be taken immediately as the rate of interest on the capital invested in the farm was "phenomenally low". In response to Farnworth's warnings the Management Committee investigated the potential sale value of the farm. The annual value of the farm was £41 1s 9d including 47½ sheep gaits (see Appendix 5). At a 20-year purchase value, the sale of the farm would raise only about £820 and, even if the Society was fortunate enough to get a 30-year purchase value, the farm would raise only £1,230. Having discovered that the valuation was so low, the Management Committee took the view that land prices were eventually bound to rise again and decided not to sell.

> TELEGRAMS.
> KING, EDGLEY,
> AYSGARTH,
> 2 MILES.
>
> EDGLEY,
> LEYBURN. R.S.O.
> YORKSHIRE.
>
> 26 March 1901
>
> Dear Mr Whaley –
>
> Askrigg Club Farm
>
> I was quite prepared for your Committee to think my valuation a low one but at the same time do you think any one will give any more for it – The value of a property is the amount you can get for it – and I quite think it will have to be sold cheap to get a customer and I am not at all sure that a purchaser can be found at all.
>
> Yours faithfully
> T W Firbank King
>
> The Rev.
> C Whaley
> Askrigg

Correspondence concerning Shaw Farm valuation, 26 March 1901

The farm continued to cause problems. Not only was the rate of return low but the Society had to pay an annual tithe rent charge to Trinity College, Cambridge for sheep gaits. This payment varied from year to year but the charge generally was rising. For example, in 1881, 5½d per gait was charged which resulted in an annual rent of 19s 7d; by 1904, the charge had risen to 1s per gait and the annual bill was £2 7s. In addition, between 1900 and 1902, the Society paid John Atkinson £2 10s per year for repairs he had undertaken on the farm. Atkinson felt that £2 10s should be an automatic rebate and kept this amount back from his 1903 rent payment. This was the final straw and the Management Committee demanded the outstanding £2 10s from Atkinson. There is no record of the outcome of this stand-off but the Society had had enough and decided, at last, to heed Mr Farnworth's advice. Shaw Farm was put up for sale and in 1904 was eventually sold to Matthew Williams.[5] So ended a rather sad investment episode for the Society which, given the many members who were associated with farming, must have served to emphasise the problems of dales farmers as they struggled to survive the difficult years of depression.

Surprisingly, after all the problems at Shaw Farm, some of the Society's funds still continued to be used for real estate. For example, a loan was given to an individual, presumably an AEBFS member, for a property in South Shields. However, once again, this type of investment was not successful and in 1916 the Society called in the loan.

Abbotside Common sheepgait receipt, 1903

It is not clear how the proceeds from the sale of Shaw Farm were invested, but farming obviously held no attraction and there is no record of any further investment in agricultural land. In 1905, the Society invested £50 "upon real securities" but no detail is given of the investment. In the early years of the First World War the Society de-

---
5 Unfortunately, the sale price was not recorded.

cided to support the war effort and invested £400 in War Loan stock This was felt to be a sound decision and, in 1925 and 1933, two further sums were invested bringing total funds in War Loan stock to £675. In response to the crisis of the Second World War, the Society decided, in 1941 and 1942, to 'invest' £125 and £175 respectively in the Askrigg War Weapons Week Fund. It appears that despite being called an investment, these were donations as part of the village's war effort.

War Loan stock continued to be held by the AEBFS until the 1950s when Mr Lane, the actuary, advised that this type of stock was declining rapidly in value and suggested that the stock be sold. The Management Committee gave the advice some consideration but decided to keep the stock. In 1959 Mr Lane pointed out that the Society's holding in the War Loan at 3½ per cent was worth only £1,007 against a book value of £1,513. The actuary sought to limit the damage to the Society's funds by factoring the continued depreciation of the stock into his valuations of its assets. In this way a reasonably realistic picture of the Society's funds could be presented. By 1969, the capital value of the War Loan stock had worsened with its value having fallen to £715. However, at this date Mr Lane offered different advice. Although the value of the stock was low, the rate of 3½ per cent interest was still being paid. He suggested it would be better to wait for a few months to see if interest rates fell and then a better price might be got for the sale of the stock. However, the improvement did not occur.

By 1974, the stock had collapsed in value to only £357 and in 1981, after much careful thought, the Society finally cut its losses. It sold the War Loan realizing £546, which was a book loss of £967. However, this did not adversely affect the Society's balance sheet as, following Mr Lane's action in 1959, the value of the stock had continued to be written down.

In addition to its War Loan stock, the Society had a holding of 7 per cent British Savings Bonds. It decided to dispose of this investment progressively in 1977 and 1978, and to invest in the higher yielding Local Council Bonds. As a result of sales of various stocks and bonds, in 1981 the Society was able to invest £5,400 in short-term bonds with local authorities and, in addition, held some £3,700 in high yielding deposit accounts, mostly with the National Savings Bank. This careful management of the funds, coupled with continuing, relatively low payments for benefits, meant that the quinquennial solvency rate of 89p in the £ in 1969 had risen to 152p in the £ in 1984. The purchase and sale of different stocks and bonds on the advice of the actuary and others, continues to the present day as the Management Committee seeks to obtain the best return on the Society's investments consistent with security.

Outgoings

For most of its existence the Society has had three main calls on its funds: payment of benefits, running costs and social events.

1895					£	s	d
Feb:25 – June 8	To Ed. Tiplady 14 w:	Sick Allowance	@5/-		3	10	0
Feb:25 – Mch 4	" Chris Blades 1 w	" "	@5/-			5	0
Feb:25 – June 8	" Wm. Ashbridge 14 w:	" "	@5/-		3	10	0
Mch:1 – May 31	" Frans Walker 13 w:	" "	@5/-		3	5	0
Mch 26 – Ap.16	" Geo. Tiplady 3 w:	" "	@7/-		1	1	0
May 9 – 16	" Alex. Metcalfe 1 w:	" "	@7/-			7	0
Feb:26 – Mch 26	" Geo. Tiplady 4 w:	" "	@10/6		2	2	0
Mch:13 – 20	" John Airey 1 w:	" "	@10/6			10	6
Mch:25 – April	" John Airey 1 w:	" "	@10/6			10	6
April 11 – May 9	" Alex. Metcalfe 4 w:	" "	@10/6		2	2	0
May 3 – 13	" Wm. Caygill 1½ w:	" "	@10/6			15	0
May 3 – 31	" John Milner, Bainbridge 4 w:	"	@10/6		2	2	0
May 20 – June 2	" Thos. Cockburn 1⅚ w:	" "	@10/6			19	6
March 8	" Funeral Allowance: the death of C Blades				4	0	0
May 15	" " " the death of John Storey				4	0	0
May 28	" " " to A Kirkbride on death of wife				3	0	0
May 21	" Tithe Rent Charge					14	10
June 8	" Bonus to Geo. Milner					5	0
June 8	" Rent of Club Room					5	0
June 8	" Postage etc					6	2
					43	0	6
	Balance in Treasurer's hands				154	19	6
	Chris Whalley				198	0	0
	President						

Statement of AEBFS Expenditure, June 1895

From a very early stage, it was clear that all three elements were important but, in order to protect its capital, the Society has always tried to meet its annual commitments through current funds. Table 4.5 shows the outgoings of the Society which relate to its 'local' management costs.

Table 4.5

Outgoings of the AEBFS at Intermittent Dates between 1813 and 1989[1]

	Sickness and all other Benefits £	Management Costs £	Social £	Total Outgoings £
1813	9	--	10	19
1821	11	3	15	29
1830	19	5	10	34
1859	92	--	--	92
1890	82	7	2	89
1900	122	--	--	122
1909	79	6	2	85
1916	95	6	2	121
1920	36	6	2	42
1929	24	7	2	31
1940	26	1	4	31
1941	21	7	3	31
1949	61	7	7	75
1969	142	40	7	189
1979	112	72	3	187
1989	137	119	24	280

[1] To nearest £ at current prices.
[2] Not recorded separately from Management.
Note: Some 'Social' may have been recorded in 'Management Costs' section.
Source: See Table 4.3.

By the late nineteenth century, other 'external' costs were being incurred, such as Friendly Society Registration, and fees for actuarial and accountancy services. As the Table shows, the level of support given in benefits compared with the costs of management and social activities varied hugely over the period. In 1830 and in 1989 benefits and other costs each comprised about half the total outgoings. However, in 1900 all recorded outgoings were spent on benefits and in 1969 benefits comprised 75 per cent of total outgoings.

In the 1990s, in the light of changing circumstances and the heavy costs of national registration as required by the Life Assurance & Unit Trust Regulations Organization (LAUTRO), the AEBFS benefit system was radically changed. In 1993 Society members decided that they could no longer afford the annual membership fee of LAUTRO. As a result of its consequent deregistration, the Society was precluded from paying death and 70-year old endowment benefits. All existing members received, in lieu of death benefit and 70-year old endowment benefit, a 'present value' benefit payment related to their age and length of membership. A consequence of the withdrawal from LAUTRO was that the AEBFS could no longer operate as a legally bound sickness benefit society. However, to retain the spirit of the Society's original purpose, it was agreed that sickness benefits would still be paid but that the payment would be discretionary. Members noted that, despite the discretionary clause, it was the intention always to honour legitimate claims for sick benefit.

Throughout its existence the Society has had to juggle with the complex mix of income and expenditure in an attempt to maintain viability. This 'mix' has included members' subscriptions; returns on investments; calls on funds from sickness, death and the 70-year old endowment benefit; local management costs; national registration fees; and valuation fees. That the AEBFS has succeeded in doing this and still 'staying in business' to serve its members, despite fluctuating membership and occasional less-than-successful investments into 'real estate', is due largely to the commitment of its Management Committee.

Chapter 5

In Sickness . . .

In the nineteenth century and for much of the twentieth century, fear of poverty was never far away from most manual workers. Even those who worked as craftsmen could, after a few weeks of sickness during which they were deprived of the weekly income, find themselves and their families threatened with pauperism. There was, therefore, a strong incentive to join a friendly society in order to provide insurance against sickness and death.

Benefits

To ensure that their members were adequately protected friendly societies had to calculate, employing actuarial methods, the likelihood and frequency of claims arising from members and adjust the level of benefit and income accordingly. Many societies, particularly in the early nineteenth century, miscalculated the risk, possibly suffering unexpectedly high sickness rates, and went bankrupt. The AEBFS was fortunate in being able to maintain a judicious balance between a relatively low subscription level and worthwhile benefit levels, because Wensleydale was, generally, a healthy place to live and many local people enjoyed longevity.

As Table 5.1 confirms, the actual level of sickness and the number of deaths in the AEBFS was usually lower than the expected level calculated on the basis of actuarial tables. Mr Farnworth, the actuary, in 1890 put this down largely to 'the healthy occupation of the members in rural districts'.

Table 5.1

Expected and Actual Sickness and Death 1886-90 to 1985-89[1]

	A	B	C	D	E	F
1886-90	488	419	86	13	11	85
1896-1900	597	481	81	16	10	62
1920-24	391	87	22	13	4	31
1954-59	279	148	53	3	3	100
1980-84	1665	749	45	8	5	63
1985-89	[2]	[2]	19	10	8	80

A – Sick pay "expected" in £s
B – Sick pay "actual" in £s
C – "Actual" as a % of "expected"
D – Number of deaths "expected"
E – Number of deaths "actual"
F – "Actual" deaths as a % of "expected"

[1] At selected dates over quinquennial periods – 1989 was the final valuation for the AEBFS.
[2] Information not available.
Source: AEBFS, 3/6, Quinquennial Valuations, 1886/90 – 1985/89.

Other than very occasionally, when actual deaths exceeded expectations (such as in 1949 when there were seven deaths as opposed to the four "expected"), the positive disparity between "expected" and "actual" was sometimes quite spectacular. For example, in 1920-4 the cost of sickness was 78 per cent less than expected and actual deaths were 69 per cent lower than expected. In 1985-9 the cost of sick benefits, at 81 per cent less than expected, was even more striking.

Although new members could not claim benefits during the first eighteen months of membership, thereafter all members were afforded some protection against ill health and other difficulties. Table 5.2 gives details of the range of benefits in 1832 and 1969. In the nineteenth century the level of benefit provided protected members from pauperism or a pauper funeral but by the late twentieth century the significance of benefits had changed, largely becoming a supplement to other support.

Table 5.2

Detailed Benefits, 1832 and 1969

	1832	1969
Ill and off work	4s pw	40s pw[1]
Ill and in bed	7s pw	
Blindness	2s 6d pw	7s pw
On decease of wife	£1 10s 0d	£5 0s 0d
Death of member up to 10 years (payable to heir)	£1 10s 0d	£6 0s 0d
Death of member 10-20 years (payable to heir)	£2 10s 0d	£6 0s 0d
Death of member 20+ years (payable to heir)	£4 0s 0d	£6 0s 0d
Amount payable on reaching the age of 70	2s pw	£5 0s 0d

[1] The benefit was reduced after 4 weeks to 10s per week for the next 4 weeks and then to 5s per week.
Source: AEBFS, 1/1/1; 1/1/6, Articles of the AEBFS, 1832 and 1969.

Although benefits covered a range of needs, the Society had to protect its funds as much as possible. Strict rules were imposed to ensure that only 'legitimate' reasons for benefit claims were allowed. For example, the 1832 rules state that members were not eligible for benefit if their disability was caused by venereal disease or by fighting, unless the latter was in self defence. By 1851, the rules had been further tightened and any member in receipt of a disability allowance who was caught gaming, betting, drinking, attending a fair or market, or being away from his house at night, would have his allowance withdrawn. By 1969 the criteria for disallowance had grown longer and, in addition to the earlier restrictions, included disability caused by playing football, cricket or cycling.

It was important for the Society to ensure both that its funds were not being squandered and that people were not making fraudulent claims. In the early nineteenth century sick members who lived within two miles of Askrigg were visited by a Society Steward twice a week.

> To the Stewards of the Askrigg Equitable Benevolent and Friendly Society

I hereby Certify that *Nancy Brenkley* late of *Sedbush* in the Parish of *High Abbotside* and County of *York* died on the *8th* day of *February* 18 *65* at *Sedbush* aforesaid : and that I have no reason to attribute her death to poison, violence, or criminal neglect.

As Witness my hand this *18th* day of *February* 18 *65*

John Fryer, Surgeon, Hawes

Certificate for Nancy Brenkley, 1865

Others living further away were visited as often as possible. Anyone submitting a false claim was liable to a fine of one guinea and was suspended from receiving benefit for two years. If the offence was repeated, the member would be excluded. Stewards were required to sign a Certificate of Illness. Although many of the rules were later modified to reflect changing times, the rules covering the process of verification of illness and fines for fraud were retained until 1993 when payment of sickness benefits became discretionary. As discussed earlier, Stewards were required to ascertain that the member applying for benefit was ill. They based their decision either on a visit to the claimant or on receipt of a medical certificate of ill health. Unfortunately, only a few certificates survive which show the cause of illness. For example, on 17 October 1898 William Metcalfe, a 49-year old cooper of Askrigg, was diagnosed by the doctor as having bronchitis and being unable to work. In fact, William was seriously ill and died the following day. His family, therefore, received 1s sick allowance for one day and £4 for William's funeral.

Table 5.3 gives an overview of the changes in core benefit allowances between 1832 and 1999 while Table 5.4 shows details of how the allowances were tailored to length of sickness.

Table 5.3

Changes in core benefits 1832-1999

	1832	1851	1904	1969	1984	1989	1999
Initial sick benefit (pw)	4s	6s	12s	40s	£4	£10	£22 15s[1]
Blindness (pw)	2s 6d	2s 6d	7s	7s	--	--	--
70 years lump sum	£5	£5	£5	£5	£15	£25	--
Death of member	£4	£4	£4	£6	£20	£30	--
Death of member's wife	£1 10s	£1 10s	£3	£5	£15	£25	--

[1] £22 15s = £22.75p in 'new' money.
Source: AEBFS, 1/1-5, Articles of the Society and Supplementary Rules, 1832-1999.

It is obvious from Tables 5.3 and 5.4 that one way in which the Society maintained its financial viability during the twentieth century was by not raising its benefits in line with inflation. As noted earlier, given increasing state support, the Society's benefits from 1911 onwards tended to be a supplement to other assistance rather than providing a vital buffer against pauperism as in the nineteenth century.

Table 5.4 shows that although benefits frequently remained at the same level for many years, adjustments were made from time to time. The changes did not always improve the level of benefit. If the Society felt that its funds were being drawn on too heavily, the hard decision was taken to lower benefits. For example, in 1851 members were given sickness benefit of 6s per week. This was 1s less than members had received in the previous few years. Perhaps this reflected the fact that, in the first part of the century when the Society was new and most of its members were young, claims for sick benefit are unlikely to have been high. By 1851, many of the first cohort of members were reaching a more vulnerable age in respect of sickness and, in order to protect its funds, the Society had to adjust its benefit levels. The problem was evidently fairly quickly resolved and the original level was restored in 1857. By 1876 the benefit level had been raised again and sickness benefit was initially 10s 6d per week. Although payments had generally improved by the mid-twentieth century, it was only in 1984 that benefits were significantly increased. As both Tables 5.3 and 5.4 demonstrate, a radical change in benefit policy occurred in the 1990s. From 1993, not only was sickness the sole benefit to be retained, payment had become discretionary and assistance could only be claimed for weeks 3 to 10 of an illness.

Table 5.4

Level of Sickness Benefit at selected dates between 1832 and 1999

	1st period wks[1]	1st period Benefit	2nd period wks[1]	2nd period Benefit	Remainder wks[1]	Remainder Benefit
1832	all	7s				
1851	all	6s				
1876	88[2]	10s 6d			rest	6s 6d
1890	4	10s 6d	26	7s	rest	5s
1922	4	10s 6d	26	4s	rest	2s 6d
1924	4	10s 6d	16	4s	rest	2s 6d
1939	4	10s 6d	16	4s	rest	2s 6d
1949	4	£1	12	10s	rest	5s
1962	4	£1	12	10s	rest	5s
1963	4	£2	4	10s	rest	5s
1979	4	£2	4	10s	rest	5s
1986	4	£4	4	£1	rest	10s
1999[3]	1-2	nil	3-10	£22 15s	rest	nil

[1] Weeks' duration.
[2] Up to 88 weeks.
[3] Discretionary benefits.
Source: See Table 5.3.

New societies could not pay benefits until their funds had reached a satisfactory level. This often took several years. However, due to the high level of recruitment, the Askrigg Society was able to pay benefits relatively quickly. The first recorded payment of sickness benefit was made in March 1811 when Richard Mason, a 48-year old farmer and a founder member, was seriously ill and was given 14s for two weeks' sickness benefit. Unfortunately, Richard did not recover from his illness and when he died shortly afterwards, the Society paid his wife

£1 10s funeral allowance. In the same month as Richard's illness William Banks received 4s, one week's benefit for being ill and off work.[1] As was to be expected with any 'insurance' scheme, some individuals would be net gainers over the period of their membership while others of more robust constitution would be net losers. Even the latter, however, in the days before state assistance become universally available, would have slept more soundly knowing that a minimum level of support was available if they should fall on hard times. The total amount paid to individual members varied greatly over the 190 years depending upon the incidence of claims, the level of benefit payment operating at the time and the number of weeks claimed. For example, Robert Cloughton claimed benefit for almost all the period 1821-30 and, although for most of that time he received only 1s 6d per week, the total he received came to over £39. Table 5.5 shows examples of the wide range of benefits drawn within a thirty-year period.

Some of the men listed in Table 5.5 drew heavily on the Society's funds. Between 1866 and 1879 Samuel Halton, a labourer, paid contributions of £5 17s 6d but benefited greatly as he received sick pay from the Society of £63 5s and on his death his widow received £4 funeral allowance. This constituted more than an eleven-fold return on his contribution to the Society. Similarly Christopher Heslop, a joiner from Redmire, contributed £4 12s 6d over his nine years of membership but he was seriously ill throughout his final year and received 7s per week and his widow received £1 10s on his death. His total receipts from the society amounted to £22 8s, almost five times more than he paid into the Society.

While there are many examples of individual claims, it is not easy to gain an overall picture of the level of claims, particularly for the early years. However, it is possible to construct a profile of benefits for the early 1870s. In 1871 there were 103 members insured for sick pay and between 1871 and 1875 the Society's Secretary recorded the claims of these members.

---

1 Mason received 7s per week for 'being ill and in bed'; Banks received 4s per week for being 'ill and off work' (see Table 5.2).

Table 5.5

Contributions of, and sickness benefits received by, ten members 1850-79

Name	Duration of membership	Contributions	Benefits
J. Daykin	1851-55	£1 13s 0d	Nil
E. Mason	1851-58	£3 3s 0d	17s 0d
W. Thompson	1854-66	£5 15s 6d	£10 17s 0d
T. Miller	1856-65	£4 10s 0d	Nil
T. Tennant	1856-59	£1 7s 6d	15s 0d
C. Heslop	1860-69	£4 12s 6d	£22 8s 0d
R. Horn	1860-73	£6 5s 0d	£8 6s 0d
A. Storey	1863-73	£5 0s 0d	£3 11s 0d
S. Halton	1866-79	£5 17s 6d	£67 5s 0d
J. Mudd	1869-71	17s 6d	Nil

Note: 20s=£1=100p; 12d=1s=5p.
Source: AEBFS, 3/5/1, Cash Book, 1809-81. Analysis by J. White.

It is clear from Table 5.6 that, while most of the members did not claim any sickness benefit and over three-quarters of those who did claim were ill for only brief periods, the society suffered a significant drain on its resources from four people who claimed sickness benefits for over a year. Perhaps not surprisingly, all four men were over 60 years old: William Preston, a farmer in Bishopdale, was 82 years old; George Coles, a hosier, was 68 years old; John Metcalfe, a Bainbridge butcher, was 64 years old; and James Graham, a labourer, was 62 years old.

Long-term disability, such as blindness, was also covered by the Society's benefits. Fortunately, there were few claims for disability. For example, William Heseltine, an innkeeper who had joined in 1812, became blind in c1840 and was paid a total of £63 3s 9d until his death in 1851. Similarly, John Mason, a servant who had joined as a 22-year old in 1810, was blind for four years until his death in 1858 and received over £27 during that period.

Table 5.6

Members assured for Sick Pay and Claims Made During 1871-75

	0 weeks	1-4 weeks	5-9 weeks	10-19 weeks	20-52 weeks	53-259 weeks	5 years	Total members
Weeks sick	55	26	11	6	1	2	2	103

Note: Nine members died during the five year period.
Source: AEBFS, 2/3, Members Sickness List, 1871-1875.

The benefits paid to members when sick did not fully compensate them for loss of earnings. For example, in the second part of the nineteenth century, when agricultural wages in Yorkshire were between 12s and 16s per week, the Society's weekly benefit was only 7s. The benefit payments, therefore, were sufficient only to prevent members from falling on such hard times that they were forced to claim poor relief and, possibly, be sent to the workhouse in nearby Bainbridge. Although the benefit level was modest it fulfilled its role in providing basic subsistence and in 1844 the AEBFS was able to claim that over the previous 30 years none of its members had applied for poor relief.

Death

In addition to the fear of sickness and falling into pauperism, many working class people were terrified of being unable to pay for their own funeral and, consequently, of being buried in an unmarked pauper grave. Burial clubs became increasingly popular during the nineteenth century as people sought to ensure that funeral expenses would be paid. In common with many friendly societies, the AEBFS rules prevented its members from joining other benefit societies. This restriction included burial clubs. It was, therefore, incumbent upon the AEBFS to ensure support for burial and to this end the Society offered a lump-sum death benefit. As with the sickness benefit, the Society's payment on death was not generous but was designed to support funeral costs. As the average cost of an adult burial for the lower classes in 1843 was about £4, the payment of £1 10s death benefit to new Society members would not have been sufficient to cover costs. However, members of over 10 years received a death benefit of £4 and, therefore, could expect a 'respectable' burial.

CERTIFICATE OF THE DEATH OF A PERSON

(Friendly Societies Act, 1875; - Friendly Societies Amendment Act 1876)

Superintendent Registrar's District of _Middlesborough_

Registrar's Sub-District of _Thornaby_ in the County of _York_

When and where Died	Name and Surname	Age	Rank or Profession	Cause of Death	Signature, Description and Residence of Informant	When Registered	Signature of Registrar
Sixth October 1882 8 Barnard Street Thornaby South Stockton U.S.D	John Thompson	47	Timekeeper at Ironworks	Phthisis Pulmonalis certified by John Dale M.R.C.S	Ann Thompson widow of deceased present at death 8 Barnard St. Thornaby	7th Oct 1882	George Sanderson Registrar

Given under my hand this _7th_ day of _October_ _1882_

GHO Sanderson
Registrar.

Certificate of Death, 1882

The death benefit was one form of insurance which all members of the Society, or their families, claimed at some time. The burial allowance was given for the deceased member or his next-of-kin, which could include mothers and siblings etc., as well as wives. Certificates of Death, signed by the Medical Attendant or the Registrar, were required before the Society would release the death benefit. The next-of-kin, who received the death benefit, had to acknowledge in writing receipt of the allowance. Most of the death certificates were on a specially printed form but some were hand written. All had to affirm that the death was not due to poison, violence, or criminal neglect. The first burial allowance was given in March 1811 to Margaret Hanson on the death of her husband. Later in the same month, Anthony Storey received £1 10s on the death of his wife.

> June 4/1904
>
> Dear Preston I have received my Fathers club money allright and got it cashed with thanks for you sending it on to us
>
> Yours truly
> James Ashbridge
> 14 Harrison St
> Burnley Wood
> Burnley

Letter acknowledging receipt of Death Benefit, 1904

While many members lived to a good age, there were some, as shown in Appendix 6, who died young. All death certificates had to be witnessed by next-of-kin or close acquaintance. However, even by the late nineteenth century there were quite a few people who were unable to write their own name. For example, Robert Thompson put his mark, X, on the death certificate to state he had been present at John Preston's death in 1888. Eleazor Chapman, the Askrigg Registrar signed the certificate confirming Thompson's mark.

Askrigg Equitable Benevolent and Friendly Society

Received this day from the Treasurer and Stewards of the above Society the Sum of *One pounds and Ten Shillings* being the Burial allowance due from the said Society, on the death of my late *Wife, Nancy Brenkley of Sedbush* to me as h *er Husband* and next of kin, in accordance with No. 18 of the said Societies' Rules.

As Witness my hand this *18th* day of *February* 18 *65*.

Thomas his mark *Brenkley*

Witness.
John Fawcett

Receipt for Burial Allowance, 1865

Sometimes, cause of death was closely related to the type of occupation followed. Life for local farmers has always been difficult and farming was arduous work. It is not surprising, therefore, that exhaustion was cited as part cause of death on Robert Cloughton's certificate (see Appendix 6). Similarly, 50-year old James Sedgwick Peacock, a Bainbridge coal merchant, died in 1945 of chronic asthma and heart failure.

Clearly, in the nineteenth century, medicine was not advanced and examples shown in Appendix 6 demonstrate that many members and their next-of-kin died from relatively simple ailments. For example, Israel Carter Storey, a 26-year old police constable, died in Leyburn in 1877 of a strangulated hernia, while Mary Milner and Sarah Little both died from childbirth related problems. Sarah had survived for one day after the birth but suffered a haemorrhage and convulsions. Where a person died without an obvious cause, an inquest was held. In 1896 Francis Metcalfe, a 52-year old railway plate-layer was deemed at inquest to have died of natural causes at Low Abbotside;

while in 1901 an inquest recorded a verdict of suicide by hanging on William Smith, a 53-year old farmer of Thornton Rust.

Most people died in a private house, usually their own home. Some, such as John Banks, though not paupers, were given medical attention in the Poor Law Union Workhouse which, as was often the case in remote areas, doubled as an infirmary for any sick person when necessary. From the early twentieth century people were increasingly treated in the nearest hospital which was some thirty miles away. The treatment was not always successful. For example, 66-year old Mary Cloughton died in 1903 of intestinal obstruction at the Cottage Hospital, Northallerton.

As Table 5.7 shows, by the time of death a significant number of the Society's members had moved elsewhere in the country. One of the main places which attracted Wensleydale people was the Burnley and Colne areas of Lancashire, while the West Riding, particularly Bradford, and the Durham and Teesside areas were also popular destinations. Peter Storey, for example, who had joined the Society in 1820 died in Durham in 1865, and Edward Tiplady, a plate-layer, died in Stokesley in 1901. William Ashbridge, who had been a carter, moved residence to Burnley where he died of bronchitis at the age of 59 in May 1904. William Dinsdale, a foreman joiner, died in South Shields in 1903 at the age of 43.

Table 5.7

Places of Death of AEBFS members or kin 1867-1945[1]

Askrigg	62
Bainbridge	28
Elsewhere in Wensleydale	34
Bradford and Leeds	5
Burnley and East Lancashire	9
North East	11
Elsewhere in England	17

[1] Information taken from extant records. Details of all deaths over this period have not survived.
Note: See Appendix 6 for full details of some individual members.

When Society members moved to new areas they often changed occupation (see Appendix 6 for details). For example, Nathan Burton Clapham had joined the Society in 1879 as a 19-year old labourer in Askrigg. Shortly afterwards he had moved to Kirkdale in Lancashire where he worked as a coachman. However, he still kept up his friendly society subscriptions and so in 1887, when his 24-year old wife died, he was eligible for the burial allowance.

Medical Attendants

For the first 30 years of the Society's existence, the validity of claims for sick benefit was determined by the Society's Stewards. In 1845, however, members decided to appoint a doctor and agreed to ask Thomas Parke, a local surgeon, to be the Society's Medical Attendant on an annual remuneration of 2s per member. Parke was required to attend to the sick members who lived within five miles of Askrigg and administer such medicines as were needed. Members who lived further than five miles from Askrigg were required to pay the doctor's travel costs. It was agreed that the medical services would be optional and that, while the Society would pay 1s per head of the doctor's fees, members opting into the scheme would be required to pay an additional 1s per annum to the Society. Although, as noted earlier, honorary members could not draw sickness benefit, they were allowed to avail themselves of this service.

The new system appeared to work well until 1884 when Dr Baker, who had been the Society's doctor since the mid-1870s, informed the Society that he would not be able to continue in the post of Medical Attendant for less than 3s per member. He acknowledged that the Society was welcome to approach other doctors if it wished. The Society had been very satisfied with Dr Baker's work in the past and decided to retain his services. Although the doctor's fee was raised to 3s, it was decided that the extra cost of 1s should not fall on the Society but upon individual members who, in future, would contribute 2s. The level of total fees paid to the doctor varied from year to year. For example, Dr Baker received medical fees amounting to £18, £15, £15 6s, and £14 17s in 1885, 1889, 1892 and 1899 respectively.

By 1913 the fees had risen significantly and the doctor was paid 8s 6d annually per member including medicines.

Table 5.8

Doctors of the Society 1845-2000

1845	Mr Thomas Parke (surgeon)
c1875	Dr Baker
1905	Dr Hime
1914	Dr Dunbar
1919	Drs Dunbar and Pickles jointly
1935	Drs Pickles and Ord
1945	Dr Pickles
1948	Drs Pickles, Coltman and Coltman
1965	Drs Coltman and Coltman
1981	Drs Hoyle and Hoyle
1996	Upper Wensleydale Medical Practice

Source: AEBFS, 3/5/1, Cash and Minute Book 1809-81; 2/7, Minute Book, 1881-2000.

Immediately after World War I Dr Dean Dunbar, who had been the AEBFS Medical Attendant since 1914, expanded his upper Wensleydale practice to include a second doctor. The Society felt it would be helpful to have both practice doctors in their service and appointed the new doctor, Dr Will Pickles, as a second Medical Attendant. In 1948 the Society broke its male tradition and appointed both Dr Bernard Coltman and his wife Dr Katherine (Kit) Coltman as Medical Attendants. Obviously, Kit was not a member of the Society even though all the other doctors, with the exception of her husband, had been honorary members. The situation was the same for Dr Margaret Hoyle when she was appointed in 1981, even though her husband, Dr Derek Hoyle, was an honorary member. As Table 5.8 shows, the doctors gave the Society many years' service: Dr Dunbar served for 20 years; Dr Pickles for 45 years; and the Drs Coltman for 32 years.

'Seventy-Year Old' Bonus

Throughout the history of the Society until 1993, although members paid subscriptions only until the age of 70 years, benefits could still be claimed after reaching that age. The earliest record of members attaining 70 years was in December 1820, when both James Pratt and Jeffrey Dinsdale reached 70 years and, therefore, were relieved from paying subscriptions.

Given the health of dalesmen, it is clear that the expectation was that a 70-year old would probably continue to work and, if possible, earn a reasonable wage. In the early years of the Society, the Articles stipulated that if the 70-year old was too infirm to earn at least 5s per week, the Society would provide a weekly pension of 2s. It is clear from this rule that anyone earning less than 5s a week was considered to be in danger of pauperism. In the early years of the nineteenth century, local outdoor labourers were paid between 10s and 12s per week, so the 2s weekly pension provided only very minimal support for the lowest earners in the Society. However, even 2s appears to have been too high for the Society's resources. Given the longevity of many members, the 70-year old weekly pension was causing a heavy drain on the Society's funds and, in 1838, the weekly pension was replaced by a single bonus of £5. As a further refinement to the rules, a member was only eligible for the 70-year old bonus if he had not claimed more that £30 in benefits during the whole period of his membership.

People in the nineteenth century were often unsure of their exact age and careful checks on the age of 70-year old claimants of the bonus sometimes highlighted errors. For example, in 1844 a discrepancy came to light concerning the age of George Broderick. The date of birth entered in the Baptismal Register did not tally with the age he gave when joining the Society. The Committee decided he should still receive £5 when he reached 70 years but that he was to pay an additional 10s into the Society's fund for five years to cover his mistake.

Annual Costs of Benefit

Although, as has been shown in Table 5.1, the actual costs of benefit payments were usually less than actuarial predictions, nevertheless, as Table 5.9 demonstrates, on occasions, costs were quite high. The highest year for sick pay in the nineteenth century, noted in Table 5.9, was 1886 when £122 was paid out. There is no indication as to why the payments should be so high at this date. However, nationally there were outbreaks of typhoid in the early 1880s.

Table 5.9

Annual Costs of Sickness and other Benefits (1811-1999)[1]

	Total sick pay £	70 year endowment £	Death £
1811	5	nil	3
1815	2	nil	1 10s
1830	13	nil	7
1850	25	nil	1 10s
1886	122	nil	18
1890	64	5	4
1900	98	14	10
1905	63	5	15
1916	91	nil	4
1925	19	6	nil
1931	18	3	6
1945	30	5	18
1950	53	nil	12
1969	137	5	nil
1979	106	nil	6
1989	92	45	nil
1999[2]	273	N/A	N/A

[1] For selected years to the nearest £.
[2] From 1993 the benefit for death and the 70-year old bonus were no longer given.
Source: See Table 4.3.

As noted earlier, there were few claimants of the 70-year endowment benefit in the early years and, thereafter, the payment fluctuated. Several members must have reached their seventieth birthday in 1989. The annual cost of benefit payments fluctuated wildly from year to year. For example, in 1998 benefit payments had totalled £881 whereas in 1999 they were a modest £273.

The annual cost of benefit payments to members, as shown in Table 5.9, may not appear great but for individual members the benefits received, particularly in the years before the introduction of state assistance, provided welcome support. However, as the next chapter demonstrates, benefits were not the only reason for joining the Society and for many the social activities formed an important part of the reason for being an AEBFS member.

Chapter 6

. . . and in Health

Social

In addition to providing support for the physical wellbeing of members, friendly societies offered the opportunity for socializing. This was particularly important for members living in rural communities which were often isolated and where the daily work was, normally, a lonely activity. In addition to socializing, societies sometimes offered an economic advantage. Meetings provided a forum in which many men from all walks of life could meet, exchange views and perhaps help each other, either in business or by offering employment. Indeed, one of the rules of the original Wensleydale Union Society stated that:

> It is recommended to every Member of this Society, to give Preferences, so far as it may be convenient, to his Brother-Members, in their respective Trades and Occupations.

Although this rule was not carried forward to the Askrigg Society, the social element of the AEBFS was very important for most members.

In common with many other friendly societies, the Askrigg Society met at a local pub, the King's Arms Inn in Askrigg, and had the use of the special, adjoining, 'Club Room'. For most of the nineteenth and twentieth centuries the Society paid an annual rent of £5 to use the Club Room for its four quarterly members' meetings and for any Management Committee meetings. The Society was, generally, very pleased with their accommodation at the King's Arms but, occasionally, there were complaints. For example, in the late twentieth century members frequently found the Club Room very cold in winter and in 1978 requested a warmer room for the December meetings. Mr Wormald, the landlord, readily agreed to this request and expressed the wish that the Society would continue to use the Inn for their meetings. In 1981 the King's Arms underwent extensive alteration and the Club Room was converted for other purposes. However, the Society was assured that its Annual General Meeting would not be adversely affected and, indeed, the Society continued to hold its meetings at the Inn without further disruption for another 20 years. In the late 1990s, there was serious concern about the future of the Society's meeting place when Holiday Property Bond Ltd purchased the King's Arms Inn as part of its redevelopment plans for nearby Lodge Yard. Members were greatly relieved when, after negotiations, the new owners of the King's Arms assured the AEBFS of accommodation for all its meetings for the next 125 years.

Although, throughout its history, the stated purpose of quarterly meetings has been to deal with the Society's business, it is the social element which has been the main attraction for many members. The dates of meetings, at which all members are expected to attend, are determined by the Articles of the Society. Although the original Wensleydale Union Society had monthly meetings, the AEBFS decided that four meetings a year was adequate, particularly as the Management Committee would convene at more frequent intervals. The Society's Articles determine that three quarterly meetings should take place from 6pm to 8pm on the first Saturday in March, September and December. The first quarterly meeting was in September and the fourth meeting, the Annual General Meeting (AGM), was in June. The Annual Meeting originally took place on the first Wednesday in June in order to coincide with Askrigg Summer Fair which was held on the first Thursday in June. However, when the June Fair, which had been in decline for many years, was discontinued in the 1870s, the Annual Meeting was moved to the first Thursday in June.

In recognition of the convivial nature of the evenings, a 'spending allowance' for alcohol was allowed for all quarterly meetings. In the early days this budget was in the region of seven shillings per meeting. As the cost of beer in this period was only a few pence per pint, this was quite a generous allowance for the c40 members who attended. From at least the 1820s the landlord of the King's Arms was automatically nominated as an honorary member for as long as he was landlord. John Whitton was the first such recorded landlord and he had the option of continuing as an honorary member if he retired from being landlord. The tradition continued into the twentieth century. For example, when Mr Hopwood took over ownership of the King's Arms in the 1980s, he was voted into the Society as an honorary member.

Annual Feast Day

From the very beginning of the AEBFS, the annual Feast Day was the major social item in the Society's calendar and all members living within 10 miles of Askrigg were expected to attend. The day started at 10am with a parade of members, led by a local band, through the village. This was followed by attendance at a special church service which included a sermon for which the Vicar was paid a fee (10s 6d in 1809 and £5 in 1881). Up to the 1850s the AGM took place in the morning immediately after the church service. However, later in the century this format was altered and the church service was followed by the Annual Dinner, with the AGM, sports and other entertainment taking place in the afternoon. The entertainment often took the form of singing, monologues and local dialect poetry.

It is clear that, even in the early years, it was difficult to ensure that all members attended the church service. By 1826, a rule had been established which imposed a fine of 2s 6d on all members who missed the church service without good reason. The problem of getting members to attend continued and, in 1914, the Society warned its members that the rule relating to fines for non-attendance at the Feast Day church service would be strictly enforced. By 1919 the Society agreed that the fine, now reduced to 1s, should be imposed only on those non-attenders who lived within 15 miles of Askrigg. The funds accumulated from the non-attendance fine could be quite significant. For example, in 1940 17s was collected in fines for church service absence.

In recognition of the importance of the social dimension, from its inception the Society drew on its funds to subsidise the annual feast. In May 1826, for example, members paid 1s 6d towards the dinner, whether or not they attended, and the Society contributed a further 1s 6d (raised to 1s 8d in 1837) per attending member. The cost to the Society of the Annual Dinner, therefore, was relatively quite high. In June 1819, the dinner for 72 members cost the Society £5 8s 0d and a further £8 2s 0d was spent on drinks. When compared to the £8 which was paid out in benefits to members in the previous quarter, the Society's contribution of £13 10s to the 1819 dinner was a significant outgoing.

As successive Friendly Society Acts increasingly legislated concerning the legitimate use of friendly society funds, it became clear that the Askrigg Society's subsidy of the Annual Dinner was under threat.

In 1876 members resolved to contact the Registrar of Friendly Societies and request that the AEBFS be allowed to keep the subsidy. The Society was unsuccessful and, although it was allowed to continue to hold the dinner at its annual meeting, a new rule was inserted in the Articles which stated that:

> ...no portion of the expenses shall be paid out of any of the funds of the Society, and attendance [at the dinner] shall be voluntary.

It appears, however, that the Society still gave some support. For example, in 1937 when the Annual Dinner cost 2s 6d per head, the dinner bill was £7 2s 6d for 57 members. Although members contributed to the cost, it appears that the Society paid for two bottles of whisky (£1 5s), 1 bottle of gin (12s), a case of lemonade (6s) and ale (3s 10d). In 1938 the total dinner and drinks bill was £8 5s 3d to which members contributed £4 15s. In the late twentieth century the March and September meetings were always poorly attended, often by the Committee only. As complicated issues were usually reserved for these meetings, the sessions were often long and so the trustee present would sometimes authorise the use of the Society's funds to reward members with a drink. The last date on which financial support for refreshment was given appears to have been September 1995 when £8 was granted from Society funds. This was likely to have been for drinks.

Over the years the level of support given by the AEBFS to its social functions changed significantly. As Table 4.5 showed, support for the social element in 1821 was £15 and this accounted for over half the Society's payments in that year. However, by 1941, during war time restrictions, the 'social' outgoing, at £4, was less than a sixth of the annual expenditure, and in 1979, at £3, the expenditure was a minute element of the total outgoing of £187.

With the exception of the period of World War II and its aftermath, the annual Feast Day has continued every year to the present. In May 1940, a motion was passed that:

> ...owing to the seriousness and uncertainties of the position, the Annual Dinner be allowed to lapse for this year.

```
              ASKRIGG
              Yorks.
                    June 3rd      1937
    M   Askrigg Friendly Society

           King's Arms Hotel,
              (COMMERCIAL & FAMILY)

    GARAGE.            Proprietor : J. P. HALTON.

         Two bottles of whiskey      1   5   0
         One of Gin                     12   0
         Case of Lemonade               6    0
                Ale                     3   10

         Quarterly Meetings         1   2    6
         Special Meetings
               Extra                    7    6
                                    3  16   10


               Received June 9th 1937
               J. ......
                 with thanks
```

Invoice for drinks for the Annual Dinner, 1937

The suspension continued for the whole of the war and during the post-war period of austerity. It was only in 1950, after a break of 10 years, that members decided to reinstate the dinner. They agreed to alter the pre-war format of commencing the Feast Day at 10am. Under the new arrangement members would meet at 6pm and have the church parade at 6.45pm, followed by payment of subscriptions. The Annual Dinner would take place at 8pm and would be followed by the AGM. Even with this change, church attendance was still causing problems and, in 1960, members considered altering the format of the day again. However, it was agreed to continue with the same programme and members were urged that 'a special endeavour be made for a bigger Church Parade'. Nevertheless, attendance at the parade continued to fluctuate. However, in 1977 members rose to the occasion and turned out in force for one of the Society's most important parades. This took place on 5 June when, as part of the local celebrations for Queen Elizabeth II's

Silver Jubilee, AEBFS members paraded through the village and attended the special Jubilee Church Service.

Sports

St Oswald is the patron saint of Askrigg village church and from early times the village had held a 'St Oswald's Feast Day and Sports' on 16 August. By the nineteenth century, the sports element of the Feast Day included a 'Garland' Race and the occasion had become known as the Garland Day Sports (see Appendix 7). The sports were organized by the trustees of the Askrigg market tolls who were known as the 'Four Men'. With the decline of the village market and fair days, and their final demise in the 1870s, the sports also ceased. From the late nineteenth century, the Society had held some sports on the day of the annual meeting, though these evidently declined. However, in 1921, the Friendly Society decided to revive the St Oswald's Feast Day Sports. The event was advertised throughout Wensleydale as 'Askrigg Friendly Society's Sports', and was on 'Garland Day' in August, on the nearest Wednesday to 16 August.

The sports included trotting, potato races on horseback and other pony races; 'foot races'; and the fell, or 'Garland', race (see Appendix 8). A brass band, usually from either Hawes or Muker, attended the day and in the evening a dance was held in the village Temperance Hall. The Sports Day, which was very popular among the young men of the area, was generally a success, even though the event was often affected by inclement weather. Sometime after the 1920s (possibly during the war years), the AEBFS relinquished its responsibility for organising the Sports. In recent years the Village Sports Committee has developed the occasion into an 'Askrigg Children's Sports Day' which is held on Spring Bank Holiday Monday. The ancient 'Garland' race is still run.

There is little extant information concerning the finances of the Sports day but accounts for the 1923 Sports show that £91 was collected at the gate; £10 10s was raised from tickets for the evening dance; £8 1s was received from race entrance fees; and some additional donations were received making total receipts £143 14s 10d. Prize money accounted for £79 10s 0d and other significant outgoings included £14 0s 8d for advertizing and £33 6s 8d Entertainment Tax.

Total outgoings came to £152 13s 1d so, overall, a loss of £8 18s 3d was made.

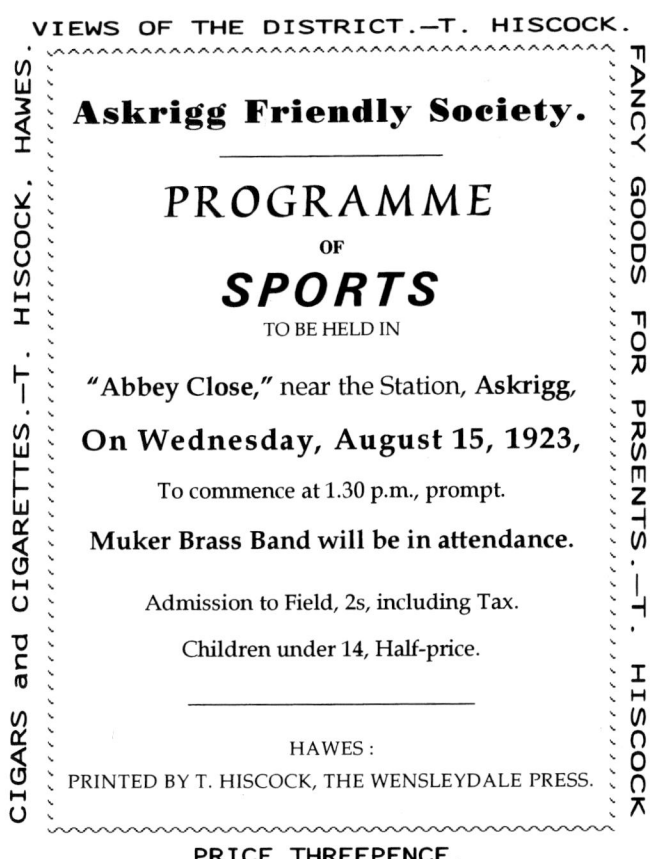

Advertisement for Askrigg Friendly Society Sports, 1923

Askrigg Children's Sports Day, 1934   Courtesy of E. Daykin

Other Social Activities

The Society occasionally held dances and whist drives for the benefit of the community. These were not always a financial success. For example, on 2 October 1929 a whist drive, supper and dance was held in the village Temperance Hall. The hire of the hall cost £10 12s 5d. The posters, tickets and badges from the Wensleydale Press at Hawes cost £1 3s 9d and the advertisement in the *Darlington and Stockton Times* costs £1 1s. A band and a piano were also hired and the Society paid for the floor to be waxed. Unfortunately, receipts from tickets sold at the door came to only £12 1s 6d. However, with the sale of food left over from the supper and donations, the Society managed to raise £18 13s 11d and breakeven.

In 1958, after the deprivations of the post-war period, AEBFS members decided that there would be an annual Society 'outing', which would normally take place each autumn. The outings were to a variety of venues and included the Ryedale Sheep Dog Trials (August 1962), football at Manchester (November 1963), and a seaside trip to Scarborough and Redcar (September 1964).

AEBFS members attending the Annual Church Service, c1985   M. Halton

The trips were always very lively and, often, were not without incident. The football match at Manchester was nearly missed because, when the coach stopped for a brief break at Clitheroe on market day, a group of members took advantage of the market-day afternoon pub opening rule. As the more sober members went in search of the group, each, in turn, was persuaded to stop in the pub for a drink while the original group insisted on finishing their game of cards. On another occasion, members visited an aggregate quarry firm and then proceeded to the City Varieties in Leeds. To the hilarity of the group watching a woman performer, one member, who must have been a farmer or butcher, exclaimed in a loud voice, 'By, she's a bit light on her quarter'. Another visit was to the shipyards of Barrow-in-Furness to view the building of the Oriana. Perhaps not surprisingly, given the members' predilection for enjoyment, the Barrow trip was 'rounded off' with an evening out in Morecambe.

In order to take account of members' interests, sometimes a choice of attraction was offered. When members visited Blackpool, some chose to watch football, while others went to the circus. One year the trip nearly did not reach its destination as a wheel fell off the bus just outside Middleham. Fortunately, the owner, who was driving the bus,

79

had another vehicle at Aysgarth so while members enjoyed a drink in Middleham, he hitched a lift back to Aysgarth to collect a replacement bus. The annual outings continued to 1967 when they were abandoned due to declining interest. The loss of interest is not surprising as, by the late 1960s, other forms of entertainment were being arranged locally and coach outings were being organized by other groups in the village. Further, many members were purchasing cars and, therefore, could travel more easily to places outside the dales.

The Society Flag and other Property

The main symbol of the AEBFS is its flag or colour. As soon as the Society was founded, members decided to have a colour made and placed an order for a silk flag with W.M. Knight of Lancaster. On 1 November 1810 Knight sent the new flag with his bill to Askrigg.

Bill for making the Colour for Askrigg Friendly Society

	£	s	d
To painting and gilding one colour on blue silk both sides	5	0	0
1 oil case cover		5	0
1 pole		1	6
	5	6	6
To Mr Knight for organizing the making of 12 yards of silk flag	3	5	0
Total	£8	11	6

Knight told the Society that although the final bill might appear expensive, it was, originally, even more costly. Because the Society had added extra words after the original agreement, Knight had had great difficulty in persuading the painter to charge £5 instead of £5 5s. The flag was so large (c7 feet high by 8 feet wide) that, in order to enable bearers to carry it, additional poles were needed. In September 1810, the Society ordered extra poles to be made, at a cost of 12s 10d, by two members, Clement Bell and Edwin Thompson, who were joiners. Knight's flag stood the test of time well but by 1881 the 70-year old banner was in need of replacement. The cost of a new colour was £4 5 2d and the Society quickly raised the sum needed by a voluntary collection among members. The new flag was put to good use and eighty years passed before the Management Committee, in 1960, noted that the flag was in need of urgent repair and was not safe to wash or dry clean. The Committee agreed to ask the local Women's Institute if they would mend the flag and strengthen the corners. However, members accepted that, even if the banner were mended, it probably would not last long, and so quotations were invited for a new flag. Discussions continued for another year and, finally, it was decided not to proceed with the order. The 1881 colour has continued in use to the present and its survival over nearly 120 years is a testimony both to its original quality and to the careful repairs which were undertaken in 1960.

Annual procession of Askrigg Friendly Society members, c1989   M. Halton

Other 'Club' property includes a gavel; rosettes (white for honorary members and blue for ordinary members) to be worn on the Feast Day; and the ballot box together with black and white ballot balls. The ballot box forms an important part of the Society's decision-making process. In order to ensure that decisions concerning important issues were taken fairly by all members, a voting system using black and white 'balls' (small cubes) was written into the Articles. This system, which continues to the present day, is used for decisions such as those concerning applications for admission to membership. Very occasionally, an aspiring member has been 'blackballed'. Other voting takes place by show of hands.

In 1979 James Dinsdale presented a Chain of Office for the President. Other Society property includes a framed copy of the 1774 Wensleydale Union Society rules and a series of photographs taken of members at different dates. These have traditionally hung in the King's Arms Inn. The earliest extant members' photograph (c1880) shows the original flag and includes the Askrigg brass band. For 170 years all the property of the Society, including the flag, was kept at the King's Arms but in 1978 it was decided that designated Trustees of the Society would look after all the property.

In 1986, in order to enhance the identity of the Society, it was decided to have 'club ties' made which could be purchased by members. However, it was not until 1991 that the design of the ties with Askrigg Market Cross and the letters AFS was finally approved. The ties, which are in three colours (red, blue or green) proved popular with members. The first batch of 150 ties was quickly sold and another order was placed.

AEBFS Flag purchased in 1881 and still in use   C. Hallas

The social activities of the Society continue to the present. Although the motor car, television and computer have reduced the isolation of the area, the Society's activities provide an opportunity for men in upper Wensleydale to meet and share a common heritage that helps retain the distinctiveness of the dales' rural life.

Chapter 7

Past, Present and Future

The AEBFS has successfully served the community of upper Wensleydale over a period of 190 years. Although its membership is confined to men, it has, indirectly, supported other local people. For example, the Society's support for sickness and old age will have frequently lessened the misery of the member's family as they struggled to survive on a low income. In some extreme cases, the benefits will have saved the whole family from pauperism while the burial allowance enabled a member, and his next-of-kin, to take comfort in the knowledge that there would be a respectable funeral when death finally came. In the twentieth century, with the introduction of state care, the provision of benefits has been of less significance for the Society's members. Conversely, the social element has become increasingly prominent, reinforcing the cohesiveness of the local community by providing a convivial outlet for its members through its regular meetings and related activities. Nevertheless, despite the change in emphasis, the Society has continued to maintain its original insurance purpose, although now on a discretionary basis.

Although, in the past, the AEBFS aided the dales' community by preventing pauperism, it also helped the local economy and society in other, albeit limited, ways. The Society has, from time to time, assisted the local economy by providing employment for local people, for example, the building repair work at Shaw Farm. Further, it has supported the village pub by holding its quarterly and Management Committee meetings there and, no doubt, boosting beer sales on such occasions! In addition, the Society has helped the local community by organising the village sports day and reintroducing the 'Garland' race.

The Society's progress through the 190 years of its existence has not always been smooth. There were times when few men joined; when investments yielded low returns; and when high expenditure threatened its financial viability. However, despite periods, such as the 1900s and 1930s, when its future may have looked uncertain, it has managed to keep going, encouraged by its members' faith in tradition and by the gritty determination to survive which is so much a part of the dalesman's character.

Askrigg Friendly Society members, 1996   John Drew

Row 1: George McArdle, Gavin Edwards, Dominic Gregson, Stephen Bell, Allen Kirkbride, Raymond Hopwood, Ryan Whyte, Martin McIntyre, Thomas Iveson, Walter Dinsdale, James Scarr, Thomas Metcalfe, Martin Fawcett, James Thwaites, John J. Percival. *Row 2*: Brian Clarkson, Clifford Rutter, Stewart Gatenby, Anthony Cockerill, James Peacock, David Scarr, Stephen Gregson, Robert Fawcett, James Holdsworth, Ian Sunter, William Banks, Ernest Alderson, Jack Thompson. *Row 3*: Thomas Kirkbride, Bruce Fawcett, William Lambert, Owen Metcalfe, Brian Brown, Neil Bowe, Leslie Alderson, Ian Harrison, Edgar Daykin, Denis Brown, Wilfred Preston, Maurice Hall. *Row 4*: David Scarr, David Harrington, Bruce Bell, Trevor Teasdale, Thomas Punchard, Roger Scarr, Richard Mudd, Denis Mudd, James Peacock, Bernard Percival, Richard Halton, Andrew Sunter. *Row 5*: James Gregson, Hugh Gregson, Paul Bell, Darren Percival, David Cockett, Stephen Cockerill, Gary Cockerill, Martin Alderson, Malcolm Sunter, Michael Alderson, Stephen Peacock, Ian Kirkbride, Nigel Thwaite, Stephen Halton. *Row 6*: David Wood, Clive Wrest, George Webster, James Connell, John Hambly, William Thwaite, Rev. Clive Malpass, William Lancaster, Stuart Huntingdon, Peter Nimmins, Thomas Bowling, Roy Arnold, David Mason, John Thompson. *Row 7*: John North, John Peacock, Dr Derek Hoyle, Robert Petty, Michael Walker, Roger Scott, Robert Nicholls, Alex Cairns, Ian Rawlings, Owen Tyson, Peter Leyland, Robert Davidson, George Crossley, Colin Gaskell.

As the new millennium opens, the issue of financial viability still continues to cause concern. The Society is responding and adapting to a changing world. It is once again actively seeking to attract young men and is devising ways of making the process of joining easier. For example, a recent decision by members means that, instead of requiring a doctor's note certifying fitness to join the Society, an applicant will be required merely to submit a written statement confirming his good health.

Apart from the perennial problem of maintaining viable membership levels by ensuring sufficient recruitment of new blood, the greatest challenge that the Society has faced in recent years has, paradoxically, stemmed from its own objectives, inherent in its status as a friendly society. Strict adherence to its original purposes requires registration with both LAUTRO and the Friendly Societies Commission. These are national bodies and apply national scales of fees for registration. These fees are set on the basis that the vast majority of bodies seeking membership are relatively large with a correspondingly large income and asset base. Consequently, fee levels take little regard for bodies such as the AEBFS which, in terms of its size, is an anachronism in a world of increasingly large insurance institutions.

The financial burden of registration precipitated the AEBFS's withdrawal from LAUTRO in 1993, in order to save both on registration and actuarial fees for valuations. The action was timely, removing the necessity of paying fees in the region of £800 per annum for which the AEBFS had received little apparent benefit. On the face of it, the 1993 decision radically changed the Society. The withdrawal from LAUTRO meant that payment of sickness and other benefits ceased to be a legal obligation. As a result of the deregistration, the 70-year bonus and burial allowance also had to be terminated. However, the original aim of the Society has been kept as sickness benefits have been retained. Although payment of these benefits is now discretionary, the Society has stated clearly its intention to honour, as far as possible, all legitimate claims. Further, and importantly, the Society has formally retained its friendly society role through its continued registration with the Friendly Societies Commission. However, even this is under some threat. The increasing Friendly Societies Commission registration fees have put pressure on the Society's funds. In 1994 the Society had paid a registration fee of £285; this rose to £360 in 1999 and to £460 in 2000. These increases have resulted in registration costs absorbing about half the annual contribution income. It is hoped that the AEBFS can find a way to defray the costs of Friendly Societies Commission registration and be able to retain its friendly society status in the future.[1]

Despite the difficulties of recent years, the Society remains a vibrant, local institution where dalesborn members mix well with increasing numbers of 'incomers' and the total membership, at over 180, is high. The Society rests confidently on its historic traditions and in the knowledge that it is one of only a very few rural independent friendly societies to survive in Britain. With continued commitment to its survival, by both its members and the rest of the local community, there is confidence that the Askrigg Friendly Society will not only survive but will increase in strength and will still be in existence at the end of the second millennium.

---

1 Suggestions as to ways to raise money for registration have included fund-raising events; a voluntary 'registration' contribution; or ad hoc collections among members.

Appendix 1

Early members of the AEBFS, 1809-11

No.	Age	Members Names	Abode	Occupation	Date of Entry
26	35	Thomas Thompson	Askrigg	Miller	May 31st 1809
27		John Terry	Askrigg		May 31st 1809
28	32	John Metcalfe	Askrigg	Badger	May 31st 1809
29	32	John Shepherd	Newbiggin	Labourer	May 31st 1809
30	25	William Kettlewell	Askrigg	Labourer	May 31st 1809
31	42	Rev. William Richardson	Camshouse	Minister	May 31st 1809
32	24	James Banks	Askrigg	Carrier	May 31st 1809
33	21	William Banks	Askrigg	Carrier	May 31st 1809
34	29	Joseph Miller	Askrigg	Innkeeper	May 31st 1809
35	48	Mr. Barnard Linsey	Camshouse	Gentleman	May 31st 1809
36	18	Matthew Thompson	Askrigg	Joiner	May 31st 1809
37	23	Christopher Lee	Askrigg	Blacksmith	May 31st 1809
38	23	John Dinsdale	Nappa	Servant	May 31st 1809
39	23	Jacob Brodrick	Woodhall	Servant	Sept 2nd 1809
40	30	George Brodrick	Nappa	Servant	Sept 2nd 1809
41	30	William Miller	Theakston	Cordwainer	Sept 2nd 1809
42	30	Christopher Hudson	Camshouse	Farmer	Sept 2nd 1809
43	22	William Thwaite	Thwaite Holme	Slater	Sept 2nd 1809
44	-	Miles Little	Askrigg	Farmer	Mar 31st 1810
45	21	Thomas Shaw	Mallerstang	Yeoman	June 6th 1810
46	28	Metcalfe Calvert	Askrigg	Servant	June 6th 1810
47	22	John Mason	Mire Garth	Servant	Sept 1st 1810
48	20	Michael Knowles	Woodhall	Miner	Oct 1st 1810
49	17	William Birbeck (sic)	Askrigg	Collier (miner)	Oct 1st 1810
50	32	Edward Hunter	Askrigg	Badger	Mar 2nd 1811
51	25	George Tennant	Aysgarth	Mason	June 5th 1811
52	27	Anthony Dinsdale	Askrigg	Labourer	June 5th 1811
53	24	William Kettlewell	Askrigg	Labourer	June 5th 1811
54	21	Francis Clapham	Simonstone	Labourer	June 5th 1811
55	30	James Dunn	Sedbusk	Labourer	June 5th 1811
56	21	Ralph Dinsdale	Askrigg	Servant	June 5th 1811
57	22	Jonathan Hunter	Nappa Scar	Labourer	June 5th 1811
58	25	C. Alderson Esq	London	Gentleman	June 5th 1811
59	19	James Chapman	Newbiggin	Farmer	June 5th 1811
60	26	Henry Chapman	Thornton	Gentleman	June 5th 1811

Note: For Founder Members see Table 1.1.

Appendix 2

Articles of AEBFS, 1832 (selected extracts)

Introduction

THAT Institution which has for its object the happiness and benefit of mankind, becomes justly entitled to the support and patronage of the public. That Friendly Societies owe their origin and establishment to motives of humanity and charity, it is very evident from the nature and circumstances of mankind in general. Man is naturally weak and indigent; he is liable to many evils which he cannot redress, and exposed to many wants which he is not able to supply. In these respects, he stands in need of the assistance and protection of his fellow-creatures; and the same helpless condition being common to all, necessarily fixes the whole species in a state of dependance upon one another. Hence we find, that they ever had recourse to society, as the common refuge of human infirmities; where, by a mutual communication of service, and interchange of good offices they might obtain those comforts of life which were not to be met with in solitude. The utility and advantage of an Institution like this, to the lower orders of Society, is very apparent, as it gives them an opportunity, by uniting their interest and strength, to produce greater effects, and to lay up in store, against the time of necessity, a more ample provision than they could do individually for themselves. Some persons, moreover, are of such inconsiderate and improvident cast of mind, that they have little or no thought of providing for future contingencies; so that such are, by becoming Members of Friendly Societies, made, as it were, involuntarily to consult their own interest, and to provide for futurity. Many, it is true, may never be reduced, from their present affluent circumstances, to the necessity of wanting relief from a Provisional Fund. But, if they wish to taste the sweets of a benevolent heart, if they wish to store up a fund of comfortable and happy reflections, if they wish to see their charity conferred upon objects really deserving – an Institution like this claims their most serious support. In short, to do good to those who can make no return is the very essence of charity, it is to possess a heart free from all sinister and selfish motives; it is such a charity as God approves and man blesses.

Finally, to give stability and firmness to this Institution, one thing is indispensably necessary, which is, that the Members should be at unity among themselves. In order, therefore, to confirm and ratify peace and unanimity among ourselves, we do hereby voluntarily associate ourselves by the name of the EQUITABLE AND BENEVOLENT SOCIETY, and to engage ourselves to be subject to the Orders and Regulations therein specified.

I	The ASKRIGG EQUITABLE AND BENEVOLENT FRIENDLY SOCIETY is formed for the purpose of affording mutual pecuniary relief to its Members, during sickness and helpless old age; as is specified more minutely in the succeeding Articles.
II	One President, and three Stewards selected annually, shall direct and manage the affairs of this Society. The President shall be appointed on the first Saturday in every March, in the following manner, viz:- One person shall be nominated by the last preceding President, and another shall be nominated by a committee of seven members balloted for that purpose, and the majority of members then present shall determine which is President for the ensuing year; but no member shall be appointed President a second time before the expiration of two years.
III	The Stewards shall be appointed to their office on the Feast-day. One of them shall be appointed solely by the President, and the other two shall be balloted for:- Any member shall be at liberty to propose a candidate, when more than two are proposed, every member shall then write the name of his favourite candidate on a slip of paper, and those two who have the greatest number of votes shall be appointed. Every Member regularly elected, refusing to serve, shall forfeit 5s; but no forfeit shall be required from those who have served any office in the Society within the preceding two years.
V	The Stewards shall assist in keeping order and regularity in the Society; they shall examine all the orders and regulations of the Society: to them shall be paid all fines, forfeitures, and contributions, of what kind soever, in trust for the Society: and by them shall be made out of the common stock all disbursements whatsoever, on account of the Society; and at the expiration of their offices they shall deliver to the Society a full and just account of all their receipts and disbursements so made.
VII	Any President, Steward, or Clerk, convicted by sufficient evidence of defrauding the Society by embezzlement of effects – of witholding or falsifying accounts, or of any fraudulent measures whatever, shall forfeit all privileges and rights of the Society, and he shall be excluded, by the erasure of his name.
VIII	A General Meeting of the Society shall be held every Quarter, at the King's Arms Inn, in Askrigg, from six to eight o'clock in the evening, from Michaelmas to Lady-day, and during the remainder of the year from seven to nine; the first meeting to be on the first Saturday in *March*, the Annual Feast to be on the *Wednesday next to Askrigg June Fair*, and the other Meetings to be holden on the first Saturday in *September and December*, and so to be continued annually. The President, or in his absence, the Stewards, when all the business shall have been finally settled, shall declare the meeting dissolved; and in that case, every member is at liberty, but subject to the rules of good behaviour mentioned hereafter.

X　　　　　At the Feast-day every member whether present or not, shall contribute for his dinner one shilling and sixpence; and a sum not exceeding one shilling and sixpence per member, taken from the Society's chest, shall be spent. At every quarterly meeting a sum not exceeding seven shillings shall be spent in ale, which shall be equally served by the Stewards, or by any other person whom they may appoint.

XII　　　　No person shall be admitted a member of this Society, who is not free from distempers and infirmities of any kind; even periodical complaints, which are wont to return at stated times; nor any soldier, or sailor, or sea-faring man; nor any person of notoriously scandalous life and conversation: and if any person obtain admission by fraudulent means or pretences, he shall, upon conviction of two credible witnesses, be excluded.

XIV　　　　No member shall be entitled to any benefits or emoluments from the box, till he has been a member eighteen calendar months. After this period, if a member by any hurt, or sickness, should be rendered incapable of following his occupation, he shall receive four shillings weekly from the Society, but, if by such hurt or sickness he shall be confined to his bed, then seven shillings weekly, it being understood in both these cases, that he is incapable of doing any thing otherwise than by verbal orders. A member of like standing becoming blind, shall be allowed two shilling and sixpence weekly, during the continuance of his blindness; the payment of these pensions to commence on the seventh day after notice is received by the President or Stewards. No person disabled by fighting, or afflicted with the venereal disease, shall be entitled to relief, except in fighting he can bring sufficient proof that it was only in his own defence, which must be referred to a committee of the members present.

XV　　　　That it may be perfectly understood what notice will be required by the President and Stewards, from persons claiming benefits of any kind from the Society, *it is ordered in all cases*, that persons shall send a written notice of their sickness, lameness, and benefit claimed, specifying particularly the nature and extent of their sickness or complaint, to the master of the house, where the Society's meetings are held, which, if sent by the post, shall be post paid. The master of the house shall be obliged to communicate the said notice to the President or Stewards, within twelve hours, under the forfeiture of two shillings; in consequence of which, if it be a notice of the sickness or indisposition of a member, residing in Askrigg, or within two miles of it, and claiming benefit thereupon, one of the Stewards shall within twenty-four hours, and twice at least every week, so long as the claimant keeps his house, visit such sick or lame member, and in case of his residing at a greater distance than two miles from Askrigg, one of the Stewards must visit him as often as convenient, or appoint any member residing near him to visit him; and on neglect or refusal, to forfeit one shilling. The

	Stewards shall pay his weekly pension punctually every seventh day, computing from the date of the notice when received, according to the true meaning of the preceding article. Every Steward failing in any of the premises, shall, for every default, forfeit two shillings and sixpence. The Stewards are to act weekly by turns; and in case of sickness or necessary absence of the acting Steward, the other must supply his place under the last mentioned penalty.
XVIII	If any member, upon weekly allowance, shall play at game of hazard for money, lay wagers, or get drunk, he shall, for every offence, forfeit two shillings and sixpence, and his allowance shall instantly cease.
XX	No person shall receive benefit from the Society out of Great Britain, except persons impressed by sea or land, into his Majesty's service, or persons balloted into the Militia after admission; and with regard to them, the attestation of any two Officers of the regiment or ship, shall be equivalent to the attestation of a Minister or Churchwardens, in whatever part of the world they shall be.
XXI	If any person shall be convicted by the evidence of one credible witness, of receiving pensions for any longer time, or in higher proportion than according to the meaning of these Articles, he shall be excluded the Society. And if there shall be reason to suspect any member or officers of the Society of fraudulent practices towards the same, and the matter cannot be cleared up, in that case, the President and Stewards shall require such person to acquit himself by oath, before the nearest Justice of the Peace; and if he refuse to make oath, he shall incur the last named penalty. And if he be convicted of swearing falsely, he shall likewise be prosecuted for perjury, at the expense of the Society.
XXII	If any member of the Society be convicted of felony in any of his Majesty's courts of justice, he shall forfeit all rights, and be excluded from the club by the erasure of his name.
XXV	Every member, at the Annual Meeting, residing within the parish of Aysgarth, or within ten miles of Askrigg, shall personally appear at the club-room, at ten o'clock in the morning, and remain till all the business is transacted, or forfeit sixpence. Every member, on the quarter-night, shall appear before eight o'clock, or cause his contribution to be paid before that time, or forfeit sixpence for every neglect. If any member on the day of the Annual Meeting shall occasion any quarrels or disturbances either within the club-room, or in the town of Askrigg, he shall forfeit for every offence, one shilling.
XXVI	The President, Stewards, Clerk, and Master of the house shall forfeit two shillings and sixpence, for every failure of attendance at any stated meeting of the Society, either by dilatoriness or absence, unless prevented by sickness, or other good cause, to be approved of by a majority of members then assembled. In case of necessary absence,

	each officer shall depute a proper substitute, and send his key in proper time, under the same penalty.
XXVIII	Strangers may be admitted at the meetings of the Society, but shall pay sixpence for their club; if at the Annual Meeting, five shillings; and if disorderly, shall be immediately dismissed.
XXX	No honorary member shall be obliged to fill any office without his own free will and consent; if he accepts office, he must be subject to all the Rules and Regulations of the Society, but in other cases he is not to be subject to any fine whatsoever, except for offences enumerated in the twenty-third Article, which shall be binding on all the Society's members.
XXXI	Every member not attending at the Annual Meeting, or sending his payment by ten o'clock, shall forfeit sixpence.
XXXIV	That every member shall produce to the President, at the Annual Meeting, a certificate, signed by himself, or cause the same to be delivered, stating how long he has been relieved, and the sum he has received from the Society's box, which the President is to compare with the Stewards' accounts.

XXXV.	I _ _ _ _ _ _ _ _ _ _ _ _ _ of the Parish of _ _ _ _ _ _ _ _ admitted a Member of the Society, the _ _ _ _ day of _ _ _ do truly and sincerely declare that I am no more than _ _ _ years of age; and that I will, to the best of my power, conform to and abide by the Rules and Orders of this Society, to the best of my knowledge.
	As witness my hand _ _ _ _ _ _ _
	
	    Signed in the presence of .... President.
	                            } Stewards

XXXVI.	In order to keep regularity, it is directed that all ballots should be by tickets numbered according to the number of Members present, and that all votes shall be by balls, black and white, which tickets and balls are to be provided accordingly; but in ordinary matters, a show of hands shall determine, unless any member object, in that case, recourse must be instantly had to the black and white balls.

Appendix 3

Presidents of the AEBFS, 1820-2000

1820-22	Anthony Storey	1866-67	Francis Chapman Esq., Thornton Rust
1822-23	John Whitton	1867-68	James Clarkson Winn, Askrigg
1823-24	James Blades	1868-69	Rev. William Balderston
1824-26	John Lodge	1869-70	Rev. Christopher Whaley
1826-28	J.A. Alderson	1870-71	John Chapman Esq.
1828-30	Richard Wood	1871-72	George Winn Jnr.
1830-31	William Lodge	1872-73	Rev. Christopher Whaley
1831-32	Mr. J.M. Bowman	1873-74	Dr. Richard Laycock Routh
1832-33	John Chapman	1874-75	Mr. Oswald Ralph Whaley
1833-36	Rev. James F. Wood	1875-76	Mr. James John Thwaite
1836-37	Thomas Parke	1876-77	Dr. Alfred Baker
1837-38	Mr. Robert W. Metcalfe	1877-78	W.E.M. Winn Esq.
1838-39	Rev. John Winn	1878-79	Capt. Francis Chapman
1839-40	Mr. James Brougham	1879-80	Oswald Routh Whaley
1840-41	Rev. James Wood	1880-81	Wm. Lightfoot Bankes Esq.
1841-42	Mr. Lightfoot	1881-82	James Grime Lodge Esq.
1842-43	Mr. Robinson	1882-83	Rev. Christopher Whaley
1843-44	Thomas Parke	1883-84	Rev. William Balderston
1844-45	Mr. James Wood	1884-85	James Clarkson Winn
1845-46	Mr. George Winn	1885-86	Dr. Alfred Baker
1846-47	Rev. Richard Wood	1886-87	W.E.M. Winn
1847-48	Rev. John Winn	1887-88	John J.G. Lodge
1848-52	George Winn	1888-89	John C.C. Routh
1852-53	Rev. John Winn	1889-90	W.E.M. Winn
1853-54	Rev. Richard Wood	1890-91	Thomas R. Lodge
1854-55	Mr. George A. Robinson	1891-92	Timothy Spensley
1855-56	John Chapman Esq.	1892-93	William Balderston
1856-57	Oswald Routh Whaley	1893-94	Thomas Firkbank King
1857-59	Mr. George Winn	1894-95	Rev. Christopher Whaley
1859-60	Henry James Robinson, Leyburn	1895-96	J.W. Lodge, Bishopdale
1860-61	Christopher Other, Elm House, Redmire	1896-97	James C. Winn
1861-62	John Robinson Esq., Semerdale	1897-98	John J.G. Lodge, Yorebridge
1862-63	Matthew Willis, MD, Aysgarth	1898-99	Oswald William Whaley
1863-64	John Chapman Esq., Thornton Rust	1899-1900	Thomas Robert Lodge
1864-65	John Augustus Metcalfe Esq., Ings House, Hawes	1900-01	Rev. Christopher Whaley
1865-66	George Winn Jnr., Askrigg	1901-02	William Balderston

1902-03	T.F. King	1955-56	Samuel Peacock
1903-04	Edward M. Hime	1956-57	James Scarr
1904-05	John Whitfield Spensley	1957-58	W.E. Scott
1905-06	Joseph Hopper	1958-59	Dr. A.F. Ord
1906-07	James Clarkson Winn	1959-60	Andrew Wilson
1907-08	Rev. F.M. Squibb	1960-61	Richard H. Widdows
1908-09	Thomas Robert Lodge	1961-62	John Skidmore
1909-10	James Clarkson Winn	1962-63	A. Kenneth Slack
1910-11	Robert William Bankes	1963-64	Peter Leach
1911-12	Timothy Spensley	1964-65	Frank B. Webster
1912-13	William Bell	1965-66	T. Frank Outhwaite
1913-14	Thomas Robert Lodge	1966-67	Charles B. Grainger
1914-15	Rev. F.M. Squibb	1967-68	Raymond Scott
1915-17	Richard Brittain	1968-69	Thomas Scott
1917-18	John J.G. Lodge	1969-70	P. Hartley
1918-19	William Balderston	1970-71	John D.C. Piper
1919-20	R.W.L. Bankes	1971-72	Richard A. Fawcett
1920-21	John J.G. Lodge	1972-73	Ian Harrison
1921-22	William Balderston	1973-74	Philip Clay
1922-23	Richard Brittain	1974-75	Ralph Dale
1923-24	Simon Hunter	1975-76	Eric J. Adamson
1924-25	Rev. J.H.J. Bayley	1976-77	Christopher Cunningham
1925-26	Richard Brittain	1977-78	John Sunter
1926-27	James Robert Metcalfe	1978-79	James Dinsdale
1927-28	William Balderston	1979-80	Lindsey Wilson
1928-29	John J.G. Lodge	1980-81	Malcolm Scott
1929-30	Richard Brittain	1981-82	Archibald Willis
1930-31	William Balderston	1982-83	George Milburn
1931-32	T.B. Milner	1983-84	George Crossley
1932-33	Thomas Robert Lodge	1984-85	Douglas Raw
1933-34	Richard Brittain	1985-86	Ian Scott
1934-35	William Balderston	1986-87	Stuart Huntington
1935-36	Rev. A. Thurston	1987-88	Roger Stott
1936-37	Henry Trotter	1988-89	Michael Walker
1937-42	Richard Brittain	1989-90	Rev. Clive Malpass
1942-43	W.C. Ratcliffe	1990-91	John Whitham
1943-44	Thomas Clapham	1991-92	John Hambly
1944-45	Richard Chapman	1992-93	Peter Leyland
1945-46	Robert Bankes	1993-94	Keith Loadman
1946-47	Thomas Clapham	1994-95	Owen Tyson
1947-48	W. Robinson	1995-96	William Thwaite
1948-49	Dr. A.F. Ord	1996-97	Robert Nicholls
1949-50	Leonard Chapman	1997-98	Peter Nimmins
1950-52	R.W.L Bankes	1998-99	Clive Wrest
1952-53	Ian Tallantire	1999-00	David Wood
1953-54	Dr. J.Bernard Coltman	2000-01	Tom Bowling
1954-55	C. Maw		

Appendix 4

Valuation Report 1890

TO THE COMMITTEE OF MANAGEMENT

The Society is to be congratulated on having made such amendments in its financial transactions, as have conspired - together with the numerous secessions, and the favourable sickness rates - to turn a considerable deficiency into a moderate surplus, during the Valuation period. Although solvency has been achieved on the Valuation basis, there remains much for the Committee to accomplish, before the future financial and numerical progression of the Society can be said to be permanently secured. Under the existing financial arrangements, all members contribute uniformly, irrespective of their ages at entry. The younger and more desirable class of members are thus discouraged from joining the Society, for under its present constitution, they must not only contribute adequately for their own requirements, but must ultimately assist in making good the shortcoming of the persons more advanced in years. It is therefore of paramount importance to the continued success of the Society, that a graduated and adequate scale of contribution should be forthwith adopted, and applied to incoming members, in strict accordance with their ages at admission.

It also seems highly necessary to direct your careful attention to the very low rate of interest averaged on the total accumulated funds during the past five years. Although the funds have attained substantial proportions, the Society has been able to realise only 1.8 per cent on its capital during the Valuation period; hence it is obvious, that unless the interest is vastly improved, a deficiency must assuredly result in the future, from the failure of the funds to realise the Valuation rate. Neither can the gradual reduction in the Society's membership be viewed with unconcern. It is clear, that unless the vitality of the Society is carefully sustained by the regular influx of healthy young members, the proportion of permanent sick must become heavier, while the percentage of the contribution appropriated for Management expenses, must have a prejudicial effect, unless the expenses can be permanently borne by the future contributions or donation of honorary members.

It must however, be admitted, that the Society has achieved a splendid success by the amendment of the rules, and the financial operations of the five years under observation and members should be greatly encouraged to deal with the further points to which their attention is herein directed, as promptly and effectively as possible, with the object of securing the permanent solvency of the institution.

I remain, gentlemen
your most obedient servant
E.J. Farnworth F.S.S.
Actuary & Accountant

20 Cannon St.
Preston, Lancashire
February 5th, 1892

Appendix 5

Valuation of Shaw Farm, Lunds, 1901

Askrigg Friendly Society

Description	Quantities			Value per acre	annual value		
	A	R	P		£	s	d
Little Shaw	2	1	22	20/-	2	7	9
North Scar	4	1	7	20/-	4	5	10
House & Little Shaw	1	3	14	20/-	1	16	9
Little Shaw		3	10	20/-		16	3
Long Dale & Barn	4	3	28	20/-	4	18	6
Low Green & Barn	2	3	-	20/-	2	15	-
New Green	4	-	14	15/-	3	1	3
Green & Hill Head	3	3	1	12/6	1	6	4
Calf Moss	22	2	27	10/-	11	6	8
Fall & Barn	2	-	32	10/-	1	2	-
New Close	3	1	38	7/6	1	6	1
47½ Sheep Gaits @ 2/6 per gait					5	18	9
A	53	·	33		41	1	9

W. H. Tomlinson – Hatllands – Appgarth.
Thos. Fairbank, Hny
Licensed Valuers
Edgley. Leyburn

Appendix 6

AEBFS: Place, Date and Cause of Death of Selected Members

Name (age at joining in brackets)	Date of Joining Society	Date of Death	Place of Death	Age at Death	Occupation	Cause of Death	Member or Next of Kin
Peter Storey (20)	31 May 1820	1865	Durham	65	Cordwainer	NK	M
Sarah Elizabeth Little	N/A	1866	Askrigg	30	Wife of Simpson Little (farmer)	Childbirth	Wife
Anthony Winington (25)	4 Mar 1843	1867	Burnley	49	Farmer	NK	M
Alexander Tiplady (19)	3 Dec 1864	1868	Darlington	23	Corn Miller	Typhoid	M
John Tiplady (18)	1 Dec 1849	1872	Long Marton Westmorland	41	Miner (1849)	NK	M
Israel Carter Storey (22)	5 Sept 1863	1877	Leyburn	36	Police constable formally Shoemaker	Strangulated hernia (60 hrs and operation 18 hrs)	M
Ralph Harker (20)	6 Sept 1859	1877	Blackburn	37	Butcher	Phthisis	M
Margaret Kirkbride	N/A	1878	Askrigg	38	Wife of Thomas Kirkbride (labourer)	Enteric fever (27 days)	Wife
Peter Drummond Thompson (23)	6 Sept 1859	1879	Leyburn	42	Post Messenger formally Miner	Heart failure and bronchitis	M
Samuel Halton (21)	1 Dec 1866	1879	Askrigg*	34	Labourer	Hip joint disease and phthisis	M
Christopher Caygill (24)	1877	1879	Newbiggin, Askrigg	25	Farm Servant formerly labourer	Septicaemia (7 days)	M
James Ashbridge (27)	4 June 1834	1880	Burnley	73	Corn Miller formerly labourer	Heart disease	M
James Woodward Coates (19)	5 Dec 1874	1880	Bainbridge	25	Tailor	Phthisis (2 years)	M
Margaret Metcalfe	N/A	1881	Beeston, Leeds	32	Wife of James Metcalfe (labourer)	Peritonitis	Wife

97

Name	Birth	Year	Place	Age	Occupation	Cause of Death	M/Wife
Richard Halton (22)	3 June 1858	1881	Askrigg	45	Hawker of Boots	Typhoid	M
John Thompson (20)	1 Sept 1855	1882	Thornaby Middlesbrough	47	Timekeeper at Ironworks formally servant	Phthisis	M
Mary Milner	N/A	1883	Thornton Rust	29	Wife of John Milner (mason)	Cold after confinement; milk fever	Wife
Thomas Thompson (22)	2 June 1824	1884	Thornaby, Middlesbrough	82	Tailor	Chronic diarrhoea for several months	M
John Banks (18)	1 Mar 1856	1886	Bainbridge	49	Farmer and Gardener formerly servant	Apoplexy coma	M
William Lambert (22)	7 Dec 1872	1887	Bainbridge	36	Farmer	Diabetes coma	M
Agnes Mason Cockbone	N/A	1887	Bainbridge	37	Wife of Thomas Cockbone (farmer)	Phthisis Exhaustion	Wife
Jane Clapham	N/A	1887	Kirkdale Lancashire	24	Wife of Nathan Burton Clapham (coachman)	Pneumonia	Wife
John Preston (23)	6 Mar 1880	1888	Askrigg	31	Farmer/cattle dealer formerly labourer	Congestion of brain and acute delirium and exhaustion	M
Margaret Daykin	N/A	1891	Askrigg	56	Wife of John Dixon Daykin (butcher)	Coma	Wife
Robert Cloughton (27)	6 Sept 1859	1894	Horrabank Newbiggin Askrigg	62	Farmer	Malignant disease of parotid gland and exhaustion	M
Edward Tiplady (23)	6 Sept 1857	1901	Stokesley	66	Railway platelayer formally Miner	Bronchitis; asthma for 8 years	M

Name	Date of Birth	Date of Death	Place of Death	Age	Occupation	Cause of Death	Sex
John Kirkbride (21)	3 Dec 1859	1902	Gisburn Forest, Clitheroe	64	Farmer formerly servant	Cerebral atheroma	M
William Dinsdale (22)	6 Dec 1879	1903	South Shields	46	Joiner	Pulmonary phthisis and tubercular ulceration of intestines and haemorrhage	M
William Ashbridge (17)	6 Sept 1862	1904	Burnley	59	Carter formerly labourer	Bronchitis	M
William Preston Langdale (23)	5 June 1873	1926	Bradford	76	Master cabinet maker formally Upholsterer	Bronco-pneumonia and cardiac arrest	M
James Percival (23)	3 Mar 1900	1927	Bainbridge	50	Labourer	Mitral regurgitation	M
Richard Mason Trotter (27)	1 Sept 1894	1930	Darlington	64	Farmer and Butcher	Heart failure and shock due to injuries sustained in a riding accident	M
Christopher Thompson (27)	2 June 1898	1930	Burnley	59	Night Watchman formally Butcher	Leukaemia	M
William Preston (19)	4 Sept 1869	1934	Bradford	84	Formally butcher and later hoist attendant at Silk Mill	Myocardial regeneration	M
Richard Mason (26)	1 June 1905	1940	Askrigg	60	Partner of Manufacturing Diary formally farmer	Cerebral haemorrhage	M
James Sedgwick Peacock (34)	4 June 1928	1945	Bainbridge	50	Coal Merchant	Chronic asthma and heart failure	M

* registered at Askrigg but died at Shildon, Co. Durham.
NK = Not Known   N/A = Not Applicable

Appendix 7

ASKRIGG FRIENDLY SOCIETY'S SPORTS,
Garland Day, 15th August, 1923.

"GARLAND DAY" is shrouded in antiquity and no definite date can be given as to when this quaint custom first originated; but the fact remains that many of the oldest inhabitants of Askrigg and Upper Wensleydale remember with what pleasurable excitement they, as children, looked forward to this event, which was an annual red-letter day in their lives and in the lives of the inhabitants of Upper Wensleydale generally. Many of these old people distinctly remember hearing their grand-parents and parents recount the stirring events which occurred on "Garland Day" in their younger days, and doubtless this quaint custom had then been in existence for many generations.

The generally accepted version of the story is that—

> *"Formerly, a lady of means who had been disappointed in love, became embittered against the male sex in general and at her decease left a piece of land (supposed to have been situate in the township of Carperby-cum-Thoresby, where there is a field still known by the name of "Garland" Close), the rental of which was annually expended in providing a "Garland" and other prizes to be run for by the young men of Askrigg up the brow of a steep hill on the north side of the village, in a pasture known as "Garland Hill", on St Oswald's Day (August 16), in order to punish all future generations of the male sex for the perfidy from which she had suffered."*

The endowment has long ago been lost, and although isolated attempts have been made in the past to revive this ancient custom, in a modified form, it had been practically extinct (until the year 1921) for the last fifty years. The present occasion is another attempt (by the Askrigg Friendly Society) to popularise their third annual Sports by holding them on the most convenient day near to the original date and by including a "Garland" race in their programme, the prize for which will be a "Garland" made by a local lady, to which has been added substantial cash prizes.

A.T. STOREY, Hon. Sec., Askrigg Friendly Society.

Appendix 8

Askrigg Friendly Society Sports 1924

Askrigg Friendly Society's
SPORTS

WILL BE HELD IN

"Abbey Close," near to Askrigg Station,

On WEDNESDAY, 13th August, 1924,

(GARLAND DAY),
To commence at 1.30 p.m.

WHEN NEARLY **£100** WILL BE GIVEN IN PRIZES

LIST OF EVENTS (OPEN).

£30 TROTTING HANDICAP RACE.
First, £20 ; Second, £7 ; Third, £3. In Heats. Entrance, 7s 6d.

£18 SCAMPER HANDICAP.
First £10 ; Second, £5 ; Third, £3. Entrance, 5s.

FOOT RACES.

120 Yards' Flat Race (Handicap). First, £6 ; Second, £3 ; Third, £1. Entrance, 2s. 6d.

220 Yards' Flat Race (Handicap). First, £3 ; Second, £2 ; Third, 10s. Entrance, 2s.

440 Yards' Flat Race (Handicap). First, £3 ; Second, £2 ; Third, 10s. Entrance, 2s.

Half Mile Flat Race (Handicap). First, £4 ; Second, £2 ; Third, 10s. Entrance 2s.

Mile Flat Race (Handicap). First £5 ; Second, £2 ; Third, £1. Entrance, 2s.

Garland Race (Fell Race). First, £5 and Garland ; Second, £3 ; Third, £1 10s ; Fourth, 10s. Entrance 2s 6d.

Entries for all events close on Monday, 4th August, to be sent to the undersigned and to whom all applications for Entry Forms should be made.

Free Admission to the Field to all competitors paying 4s. in entrance fees.

A. T. STOREY, Hon. Sec.

Askrigg, Yorkshire.

T. HISCOCK, THE WENSLEYDALE PRESS, HAWES.

Identification of AEBFS Members in Photographs

Note: All the following lists start from the top left of the photograph and move from left to right along rows. No names are available for 1929 and 1953.

1880 *Row 1*: T. Cloughton, J. Metcalfe, A. Thwaite, R. Daykin, S. Hunter, S. Little, J. Trotter, W. Tennant, E. Brown, F. Metcalfe, R. Trotter, J. Thistlethwaite, W. Metcalfe, F. Bell. *Row 2*: J. Metcalfe, T. Caygill, Rev. C. Whaley, F. Halton, R. Metcalfe, A. Metcalfe, J.T. Chapman, W. Metcalfe, R. Daykin, T. Spenseley, J. Knowles, W. Metcalfe, N. Milner, R. Halton, P. Dinsdale, T. Baynes, J. Spensely. *Row 3*: E. Burton, J. Smith, W. Balderston, T.F. King, R.M. Trotter, A. Durham, R. Cloughton, W.H. Burton, J. Kirkbride, A.T. Storey, M. Graham, J. Trotter, B. Spence, F. Walker, A. Kirkbride, W. Metcalfe, F. Walker, T. Kirkbride. *Row 4*: F. Clapham, J. Dinsdale, T. Metcalfe, J.T. Potter, C. Halton, J. Thwaite, J. Kettlewell, J. Preston, J. Hopper, C. Preston, T. Spence, J.P. Halton, J. Handley, T.R. Lodge, F. Daykin, W. Banks, G. Sykes, J. Daykin, M. Little, J. Handley, R. Hunter, A. Chapman, J. Wetherald, T. Metcalfe, J. D. Daykin, G. Cloughton, J. Gill.

1960 *Row 1*: R. Balderston, F. Percival, R. Metcalfe, J. Gregson, R. Hopper. *Row 2*: S. Bell, H. Bell, C. Chapman, B. Kirkbride, J. Trotter. *Row 3*: R. Daykin, ?, A. Lambert, J. Humble, W. Banks, R. Daykin, J. Peacock. *Row 4*: J. Halton, L. Scarr, A. Percival, J. Abraham, M. Bell, T. Kirkbride, H. Gregson, J. Scarr. *Row 5*: W. Balderston, S. Peacock, T. Metcalfe, J. Percival. G. Percival, D. Morgan, W. Robson, T. Woodmass, A. Wilson. *Row 6*: ?, ?, Dr. Coltman, P. Leach, R. Widdows, Dr. Ord, J. Banks, I. Tallantire, ?, K. Bell, D. Mudd, ?, J. Sunter. *Row 7*: A. Scarr, R. Chapman, A. Chapman, J. Banks, H. Trotter, J. Kettlewell, G. Johnston, N. Mudd.

1985 *Row 1*: A. Hill, M. Fawcett, R. Halton, J. Thompson, B. Fawcett, J. Scarr Jnr., H. Rose, B. Brown, J. Peacock Jnr., J. Thompson, D. Mason, M. Scarr, R. Scarr Jnr., O. Metcalfe, R. Mudd, R. Fawcett. *Row 2*: D. Gregson, D. Percival, W. Banks Jnr., E. Crompton, I. Sunter, N. Fawcett, R. Scarr, M. Alderson, D. Kettlewell, A. Lambert, R. Lambert, B. Horner, C. Gaskell, D. Sharp, R. Middleton, R. Lambert. *Row 3*: D. Hodgson, G. Siddle, W. Banks Snr., J. Scarr Snr., W. Preston, R. Scarr Snr., G. Nicholls, S. Bell, M. Sunter, B. Bell, D. Harrington, D. Middleton, D. Mudd, J. Holdsworth. *Row 4*: T. Kirkbride, J. Halton, J. Kirkbride, R. Hopwood, C. Malpass, J. Peacock Snr., G. Crossley, S. Bell Snr., J. Abraham, M. Walker, T. Hall-Brunton, M. Bell, J. Sunter, J. Whitham, W. Dinsdale, G. Milburn. *Row 5*: J. Matthews, H. Gregson, T. Tennant, J. Proudman, W. Metcalfe, L. Scarr, T. Bowling, B. Peacock, J. Fawcett, R. Ellis, M. Hall, E. Daykin, J. Gregson. *Row 6*: S. Cockerill, A. Kirkbride, J. Percival, R. Scott, I. Tallantire, I. Scott, D. Raw, K. Slack, R.A. Fawcett, P. Clay, B. Coltman, M. Scott, S. Huntington.

Bibliography and Further Reading

Primary Sources

Records of the AEBFS, 1809-2000
Rules of the Wensleydale Union Society, 1774.
PP, 1803-4 (175), Xlll.1, *Abstract and Returns Relative to the Poor.*
PP, 1818 (82), XIX.I, *Abstract of Returns relating to Expense of Poor.*
PP, 1831-2, XXVI, *Return of the number of Friendly Societies.*
PP, 1852 (39), XXVIII, *Registration under the Friendly Societies Act.*
Registrar of Friendly Societies in England, *Annual Reports*, 1856-1874.
P. Romney (ed.), *The Diary of Charles Fothergill 1805*, Leeds, 1981.
F. Purdy, 'On the earnings of Agricultural Labourers in England and Wales, 1860', *Journal of the Royal Statistical Society (JRSS)*, XXIV, 1861.
A.L. Bowley, *Wages in the UK in the nineteenth century*, 1898.
A. Wilson Fox, 'Agricultural wages in England and Wales during the last fifty years', *JRSS*, LXVI, 1903.
Board of Trade, *Census of Wages*, 1906.
C. Whaley, *The Parish of Askrigg*, 1890.
Darlington and Stockton Times; Richmond and Ripon Chronicle; Wensleydale Advertiser.

Secondary Sources

P.H.J.H. Gosden, *The Friendly Societies in England, 1815-1875*, Manchester, 1961.
C. Hallas, *Rural Responses to Industrialization: The North Yorkshire Pennines 1790-1914*, Bern, 1999.
M. Hartley and J. Ingilby, *Yorkshire Village*, 1956, 2nd ed 1965.
R.P. Hastings, *Essays in North Riding History 1780-1850*, Northallerton, 1981.
E. Hopkins, *Working class self-help in the nineteenth century*, 1995.
D. Neave, *Mutual Aid in the Victorian Countryside: Friendly Societies in the Rural East Riding*, Hull, 1991.